HUNGRY BRI
The rise of food

Hannah Lambie-Mumford

ℙ

First published in Great Britain in 2017 by

Policy Press
University of Bristol
1-9 Old Park Hill
Bristol
BS2 8BB
UK
t: +44 (0)117 954 5940
pp-info@bristol.ac.uk
www.policypress.co.uk

North America office:
Policy Press
c/o The University of Chicago Press
1427 East 60th Street
Chicago, IL 60637, USA
t: +1 773 702 7700
f: +1 773-702-9756
sales@press.uchicago.edu
www.press.uchicago.edu

© Policy Press 2017

British Library Cataloguing in Publication Data
A catalogue record for this book is available from the British Library

Library of Congress Cataloging-in-Publication Data
A catalog record for this book has been requested

ISBN 978-1-4473-2829-2 paperback
ISBN 978-1-4473-2828-5 hardcover
ISBN 978-1-4473-2832-2 ePub
ISBN 978-1-4473-2833-9 Mobi
ISBN 978-1-4473-2831-5 ePdf

Cover design by Hayes Design
Front cover image: Getty
Printed and bound in Great Britain by CMP, Poole
Policy Press uses environmentally responsible print partners

For Andrew and Elodie

Contents

List of figures

List of abbreviations

CFM	Community Food Members
DCLG	Department for Communities and Local Government
DoH	Department of Health
DWP	Department for Work and Pensions
ESA	Employment Support Allowance
ESRC	Economic and Social Research Council
FAO	Food and Agriculture Organisation
ICESCR	International Covenant on Economic, Social and Cultural Rights
JSA	Jobseeker's Allowance
MIS	Minimum Income Standards
NGO	Non-governmental organisation
RDO	Regional Development Officer
UN	United Nations
VCO	Voluntary and community organisations

Acknowledgements

First of all, I would like to thank the Trussell Trust and FareShare for their support of this research, for opening up their organisations for study and for their commitment to helping the project progress along its way. My heartfelt thanks also go to all the interviewees who took part in the research, for giving up their time and sharing their experiences and insights with me. I would also like to thank other volunteers at the projects I visited, who took time out of their busy days to talk to me informally and help me get a better feel for their work.

Thank you to Matt Watson, Dimitris Ballas and Peter Jackson from the University of Sheffield for all of their guidance and advice. Thanks also to Liz Dowler from the University of Warwick for her invaluable advice and mentorship in recent years, and to Rachel Loopstra from King's College London for all her help and support. Thanks to Graham Riches from the University of British Columbia for his comments on earlier versions of this work and support of my research agenda. Thanks to all my colleagues at Sheffield Political Economy Research Institute (Speri) for being a great team and for all of their encouragement through this process.

I have had the pleasure of working with and learning from many other great organisations and individuals who are doing important work in this field. I would like to thank Patrick Butler from *The Guardian*, Niall Cooper from Church Action on Poverty, Dan Crossley from the Food Ethics Council and Alison Garnham and Imran Hussain from the Child Poverty Action Group.

Thanks to the Economic and Social Research Council for the funding that made this research possible (grant reference ES/J500215/1) and for providing further opportunities to extend the impact of this research via the 2014 Outstanding Early Career Impact award. Thanks to Laura Vickers, Emily Watt, Jess Mitchell and the rest of the team at Policy Press for all their help along the way.

Finally, I would like to thank my family and friends for all their love and support, especially my parents and my sister. I don't think I can ever thank my husband Andrew enough – for reading numerous versions and providing sage advice the whole way. And thanks to Elodie, for making it all worth it.

Foreword

Is there a more vivid depiction of acute poverty than the terrifying food-bank scene in Ken Loach's award-winning drama *I, Daniel Blake*? One of the protagonists, a penniless and starving single mum, tears open a can of baked beans and in a frenzy of hunger stuffs the contents into her mouth with her fingers. This moment of acute desperation is where people end up, the film suggests, when you not only rip apart the social security safety net but also leave the vulnerable individuals who then fall through it precariously reliant on charity handouts to survive.

The food bank was a perfect location for Loach's film; it is emblematic of political and economic changes in the UK over the past decade. Most people had never heard of food banks in Britain in 2009; now there are thousands, all over the country. Food banks have been absorbed into mainstream political and cultural discourse as a kind of shorthand for poverty, the consequences of austerity and the punitive nature of neoliberal social security reform. There was widespread shock when the UK's biggest food-bank network, The Trussell Trust, began rapidly expanding at the beginning of this decade; ironic quips about food banks being a 'growth industry' in a time of recession mingled with incredulity and embarrassment that so many people in one of the world's wealthiest countries went hungry because they were too poor to feed themselves and their families.

Arguably, the initial shock at the rise of food banks in the UK (they have been around for much longer in Canada and the US) has subsided. It is entirely possible that, in media terms, we have reached a point of 'peak food bank'. The appetite for news reports from the food charity frontline has diminished through repetition; how often, after all, can you keep telling the same awful story? Similarly, public outrage at the revelations of The Trussell Trust's annual audits (which, after early double-digit increases, show the volume of food given out each year to be roughly stabilising at enough to feed more than 1.1 million people) has faded slightly. As The Trussell Trust pointed out in 2016, there is a danger that reliance on food charity has become the 'new normal'. At the margins, the state is now seemingly content to be structurally dependent on food banks – much to the chagrin of many food-bank volunteers, who feel they have been co-opted as informal partners in the social security system, their task to help mitigate the effects of welfare cuts, chaos and delays in the administration of benefits, low wages, insecure jobs and high rents. Food banks are here to stay, I suspect; the question is how far we, as a society, will tolerate the growth of food charity as a substitute for more efficient ways of tackling poverty and food insecurity. Food banks also face a choice: are they prepared to resist the temptation to expand to meet growing demand, as the UK enters what looks like a period of semi-permanent austerity.

What complicates matters is that food banks are not, in themselves unpopular (if that is the right word), although only surely the most zealous and deluded would view them uncritically. Food-bank clients may appreciate the vital support they are given, even as they are scarred by the way the food parcel they take away with them accentuates the indignity of their helplessness. Politically, we appear to be ambivalent, admiring and distrustful of food charity in equal measure. The Right – which, ideologically speaking, ought to applaud food banks' heroic 'big society' voluntarism – is often loathe to do so, because it is embarrassed by the way food handouts highlight the brutal failures of austerity. Similarly, liberals and the Left – who ought perhaps on principle to despise this demeaning, innately ineffective and piecemeal response to food poverty are also (understandably) in awe of the powerful, communitarian altruism that drives many food-bank operations. The genius of food banks – and what fuels the public food drives that sustain them – is that they give donors and volunteers alike a direct, simple and viscerally satisfying way of responding to feelings of distress and guilt brought on by proximity to poverty and inequality. Giving food to the less well-off is culturally hardwired into many of us, often through faith; perhaps what food banks have changed is the terms by which that transaction takes place, turning an annual Harvest Festival call for food gifts into a routine request to all, via the collection baskets common to many high-street supermarkets.

Why food banks arrived so dramatically in the UK and expanded so rapidly; how sustainable and equitable they are; whether they offer more than a temporary solution to the problems they purport to address; what to do with the awkward evidence that suggests charity food is nearly useless as a means of tackling systemic food insecurity; how we might reduce demand for food charity through reform of (for example) the social security system and how we might begin to come to terms with the growing problems of food insecurity are some of the vital and pressing issues considered in this book. Hannah Lambie-Mumford was one of the first to seriously examine the UK food-bank phenomenon, and she remains one of its most insightful analysts, bringing academic rigour to a topic so often distorted by political partisanship, unquestioning faith, and wishful thinking. Her work helps us not only to understand the dynamics of the food charity 'business' but also to make sense of the wider social, economic and political crosscurrents of poverty and inequality that have ushered in what journalists, seeking a neat phrase to encompass the multiple privations of austerity, will occasionally call 'Food bank Britain'.

Patrick Butler, Social Policy Editor, The Guardian

ONE

Introduction

In the context of economic crisis, recession and austerity, charitable initiatives have emerged providing food to people in need on a widespread scale in the UK. The formalisation of this provision and its facilitation and coordination at a national level is unprecedented in this country, and raises important questions about what drives need for emergency food and how best to respond to that need. This book explores the recent rise of emergency food provision in the UK and its implications for ensuring everyone has access to adequate, appropriate food experiences.

The scale of charitable emergency food provision (voluntary initiatives helping people to access food they otherwise would not be able to obtain) has grown exponentially in recent years. In 2015–16, the Trussell Trust Foodbank Network – the UK's largest food-bank organisation – distributed 1,109,309 food parcels to adults and children across the country; an increase from 128,697 in 2011–12 (Trussell Trust, n.d.a). FareShare, the UK's largest redistributor of surplus food, now provides food to 4,652 charities (FareShare, n.d.a).

These years have also been formative for the emergency food movement in the UK in terms of public profile and political discourse. *The Guardian* (Moore, 2012) declared 2012 to be 'the year of the food bank', and hunger and the rise of food banks have been the subjects of articles and segments in many of the country's leading newspapers and on numerous television and radio stations (see, among many, Boyle, 2014; Channel 4 News, 2014; Morris, 2013; Mould, 2014). In the realm of national politics, food banks have been debated in parliament, have sparked the establishment of an All-Party Parliamentary Group and were the subject of a Parliamentary Inquiry in 2014 (Food Poverty Inquiry, 2014b; Hansard, 2013; Register of All-Party Groups, 2014).

The recent growth of food charity has occurred within a context of economic austerity and welfare reform. Public sector finances have been set on a programme of cuts, some of which are yet to kick in. An agenda of extensive welfare reform has introduced caps to entitlements and increased conditionality and an ethos of individualised risk. The rise of this provision within this context has sparked a fierce political debate – one side of which argues that these initiatives represent the success of policies calling for more responsibility to be held in local communities, the other that the rise in numbers visiting food banks is due to socioeconomic failures, unmanageable increases in living costs and ultimately a broader – and growing –'hunger' problem (Conservative Home, 2012; Dugan, 2014).

The importance of studying the rise of food charity and household food insecurity

The challenge of food charity

The proliferation of food banks as a response to crisis experiences of food insecurity presents a number of concerns, necessitating more detailed research and evidence. In the first place, food charity is neither a population-wide response nor – critically – an entitlement. There are also issues of accessibility. Both in relation to how individual access to projects is managed (for example, whether people have to be referred, thresholds of need and qualifying criteria) and how projects are run (location, opening times and limitations on usage). Ultimately, charitable food-banking initiatives and other emergency food projects like them are – necessarily, given their capacity – only able to provide relief from the symptoms of food insecurity, not to address its underlying drivers (Lambie-Mumford et al., 2014).

These issues raise important questions about how to adequately protect people from food insecurity when it occurs, and what kind of policies and provisions are required to do that effectively and universally. At the same time as focusing on alleviation, however, we must also look at what progressive and appropriate prevention looks like. These issues stretch beyond the UK; across Europe, a similar growth of emergency food initiatives is raising questions about the adequacy of social policy provision (Food Poverty Inquiry, 2014c; Nielsen et al., 2015).

Emerging evidence base

In 2013, the Department for the Environment, Food and Rural Affairs (Defra) commissioned a Rapid Evidence Review of the knowledge base on key aspects of emergency food provision in the UK, including drivers of need, outcomes of this assistance, drivers of project growth and 'best practice' in provision (Lambie-Mumford et al., 2014). The review found that the evidence base was highly limited at the time, but emergent. Since then, there have been several notable studies and evidence inquiries. These include the All-Party Parliamentary Inquiry into Hunger in the United Kingdom (Food Poverty Inquiry,

2014b), the Fabian Commission on Food and Poverty (Tait, 2015) and the *Emergency use only* report by several of the UK's most prominent poverty non-governmental organisations (Perry et al., 2014). Academic research in this area has also grown in the years since the Defra review, including the publication of ethnographic studies of food charity organisations (Garthwaite, 2016; Garthwaite et al., 2015; Williams et al., 2016) as well as quantitative analyses of the relationships between welfare reform, the social security system and food-bank use (Loopstra et al., 2015, 2016).

Other countries in the Global North have more extensive evidence of the work of emergency food charities, the demand for them and their outcomes. In North America in particular, where there is a longer history of this provision, a range of studies are available (Ahluwalia et al., 1998; Berner and O'Brien, 2004; Bhattarai et al., 2005; Daponte and Bade, 2006; Loopstra and Tarasuk, 2012; Poppendieck, 1994, 1998; Riches, 2002). An evidence base is also emerging across Europe, with studies conducted in Finland (Silvasti and Karjalainen, 2014), Germany (Pfeiffer et al., 2011) and Spain (Pérez de Armiño, 2014).

Emergency food provision in the UK forms an important focus of social science investigation. Embodied within this phenomenon are many socioeconomic and political shifts that have been affecting the country in recent years, including rising cost of living, economic recession and welfare reform (to name a few). Previous evidence from other counties in the Global North indicates that emergency food projects could represent litmus tests of deeper, more embedded social phenomena, with the most vulnerable people turning to this kind of provision only when they have exhausted all their other social and economic 'coping' strategies.

A progressive approach to food insecurity and food charity

The right to food

Researchers elsewhere in the Global North have been working to apply the right to food, illustrating its analytical utility and real-world applicability (for example, Riches, 2002, 2011); however, in the UK very little published work has attempted to do so (for exceptions, see Dowler and O'Connor, 2012; Lambie-Mumford, 2013). As will be outlined in Chapter Three, the right to food is enshrined in the United Nations (UN) Universal Declaration of Human Rights and set out in detail in several key documents (CESCR, 1999; United Nations, n.d.). The Special Rapporteur for the Right to Food at the United Nations (n.d.) defines the right as:

> The right to have regular, permanent and unrestricted access, either directly or by means of financial purchases, to quantitatively and qualitatively adequate and sufficient food corresponding to the cultural traditions of the people to which the consumer belongs, and which ensure a physical and mental, individual and collective, fulfilling and dignified life free of fear.

Within this framework, adequate access to food is a prerequisite for the realisation of the human right, but is only one aspect of its progressive realisation (Mechlem, 2004; Riches, 1999). This book employs two particular aspects of the human right to food, set out by the UN Economic and Social Council (CESCR, 1999), to form an analytical framework: first, the emphasis on the adequacy, acceptability and sustainability of food; second, the responsibility on states to respect, protect and fulfil the human right to food.

A focus on the human right to food enables a critical study of the recent rise of emergency food provision, shedding light on the role of contemporary dynamics embedded within the phenomenon and its wider socioeconomic and political context; for example, increasing neoliberalisation of the political economy in the UK, retrenchment of welfare provision and powerful political discourses placing increasing emphasis on the work of the voluntary sector and communities providing support to those in need (Kisby, 2010; Taylor–Gooby and Stoker, 2011). This rights framework and the voluntary sector initiative it helps to understand thus also gets to the heart of a key current debate in social policy in the UK: what are the roles and responsibilities of the state and charitable sector when it comes to preventing and protecting people from poverty and food insecurity?

Critique and criticism

Emergency food projects embody numerous social performances, motivations and interactions, and as such could be the focus of a vast range of social science research questions. In answering different research questions, researchers would necessarily come to differing views on the nature of the provision and the ways in which it should be celebrated or criticised. For research focused on volunteer experiences, social capital, expressions of neighbourliness and compassion, such projects represent excellent examples of the ways in which local communities respond to need in their area and are often celebrated as such. However, this book is focused on the underpinning phenomenon of food insecurity and explores the nature of emergency food systems specifically. Such research necessarily engages critically with such systems given the limited impact they can have on the food experiences of the people they help. This is not to criticise or undermine the work being done in local communities – rather, it involves asking bigger questions of other stakeholders and situating such provision within a wider context of responses. Some may suggest that such analyses are luxurious; that while volunteers in local communities are working hard to keep projects going and to help those in need, they do not have the time to ask such big, abstract questions. But these are critical questions nonetheless, to which policy makers and stakeholders in the voluntary and community sector are seeking answers.

To critically assess this charitable food movement in the context of the right to food is therefore not to dismiss the moral imperatives and level of volunteer and donor time and commitment that goes into them. These organisations and initiatives represent significant amounts of goodwill, time, financial and emotional investment and the generosity and compassion of everyone who participates in them (from donors to volunteers). However, as will be discussed in the empirical chapters of this book, they also embody the neoliberal (welfare retrenchment, insecure and low paid jobs) and commercial (dominance of a small number of large food retailers) processes that bring about the food insecurity to which they are a response. Finding a constructive way of articulating critical engagement with the emergency food phenomenon has been an important aspect of writing this book.

Examining emergency food provision from a right to food perspective

This book explores the nature of emergency food provision in the UK, provides an empirical investigation into how it works as a system and critically engages with the phenomenon from a right to food perspective specifically. It assesses UK emergency food provision against key criteria of the right to food perspective, focusing on the adequacy of this system of food acquisition in relation to the social acceptability and enduring sustainability of the provision, and explores where responsibility lies – in practice and in theory – for ensuring everyone has the ability to realise their human right to food.

The specific aims of this book are to take a systematic look at the rise and implications of charitable emergency food provision in the UK, and to bring the human right to food to the forefront of discussions about food insecurity and food charity. It also aims to bring new empirical evidence and theoretical innovation to bear on a contested sociopolitical issue in contemporary Britain, and to challenge current thinking that emphasises emergency food provision as a primary response to hunger in the UK. The book hopes to achieve these aims by providing empirical evidence of an under-researched – yet extremely high-profile – phenomenon, moving the debate forward into the implications of this growth and what it means for the future and using human rights and their affiliated concepts of dignity, fairness and universality to understand how we can overcome hunger.

In doing this, it draws on empirical evidence from the two largest national charities involved in the facilitation or coordination of emergency food provision in the UK: the Trussell Trust Foodbank Network and FareShare. Extensive qualitative research was undertaken with these organisations and data was collected in two stages: from local emergency food projects in several areas across the country and at the head offices of the national organisations themselves. Over the course of a year (September 2012 to October 2013), 52 interviews were conducted.

Chapter Two discusses in more detail the rise of food charity in the UK. It provides international, historical and policy context to this rise, as well as an exploration of current knowledge relating to household food insecurity in the UK. Chapter Three sets out the key theories with which the book engages, notably food insecurity and the human right to food. Chapter Four explores the social acceptability of emergency food provision as a means of food acquisition. Chapter Five addresses the sustainability of emergency food initiatives, in relation to the availability of food to emergency food providers and the accessibility of that food to potential recipients. Chapter Six looks at where charitable emergency food provision fits into responsibilities to respect, protect and fulfil the human right to food. Chapter Seven looks at the role of the state, examining the changing nature of the UK welfare state and the impact these changes are having on the need for and shape of emergency food provision. Chapter Eight focuses on the consequences of the rise of emergency food provision for the progressive realisation of the human right to food in the UK, and offers key conclusions and recommendations for all stakeholders.

Published at a time of concern and uncertainty, it is hoped that this book can provide not only a systematic analysis of charitable food assistance but also some hope for a more progressive future. The right to food is a unique tool in this respect, reminding us that the wellbeing of every human being matters and that actively promoting this wellbeing should be a central preoccupation for all societies.

TWO

Hunger and charitable emergency food provision in the UK and beyond

The recent rise of food charity in the UK can usefully be placed into a wider historical, international and national policy context. As this chapter demonstrates, looking to the history of emergency food provision in the UK highlights that the modern manifestation of this charitable initiative is distinct from the country's long tradition of local food assistance. International food security and food charity research also provides insight into the growth of food charity in other country contexts and points to potential parallels, particularly in terms of the relationship between welfare reform and food charity growth.

Situating the rise of food charity and household food insecurity into the contemporary UK policy context highlights some of the key challenges facing policy and practice work in this area. The absence of accepted definitions and direct measures of household food insecurity means that a robust evidence base – and corresponding policy understanding – of food access is lacking in the UK. But it is the social policy context of the rise of food charity that is particularly important – and contentious. Food charity provision has grown at a time of unprecedented change in the UK welfare state, and the relationship between the rise of food charity and welfare reform is one of the most hotly contested – and politicised – aspects of this research area.

The rise and distinctiveness of modern food charity in the UK

The provision of free or subsidised food to people in need is not new in the UK. Churches and other charitable initiatives have long provided such assistance in local communities (McGlone et al., 1999). However, the last 10 years has seen the establishment and proliferation of national-scale organisations that are facilitating or coordinating this work in more formalised ways (Lambie-Mumford et al., 2014). Their professionalisation, coordination and scale make these initiatives distinct, and they have come to symbolise an increasing role for charities in caring for people in food insecurity in the UK. These organisations are therefore different from historical responses to hunger, which have been more ad hoc and localised and relatively out of the view of the mainstream media.

The two most prominent food charities in the UK – the Trussell Trust Foodbank Network and FareShare – provide prime examples of the distinctiveness of these newer initiatives. Both organisations operate on a not-for-profit franchise basis with layers of local and national management.

The Trussell Trust Foodbank Network is a network of not-for-profit franchises of the 'Foodbank' project.[1] The initiative involves the collection, storage and distribution of food to people in 'crisis' at a local level (Lambie-Mumford, 2013). Provision takes the form of food parcels containing a prescribed combination of long-life food stuffs, given to people who have been referred by professionals in the local community.

FareShare is a surplus food redistribution charity that takes surplus food from within the food system and redistributes it to community projects, which in turn give the food to people in need. Provision therefore varies depending on what the projects provide and could include, for example, hot meals or food parcels.

The recent growth and current scale of these charitable initiatives is also unprecedented for UK food charity. Both established in their current guise in 2004, FareShare reported that they redistributed food to over 1,000 charities in 2013 (FareShare, 2014); in 2014–15, the

Figure 1: Trussell Trust food parcel distribution

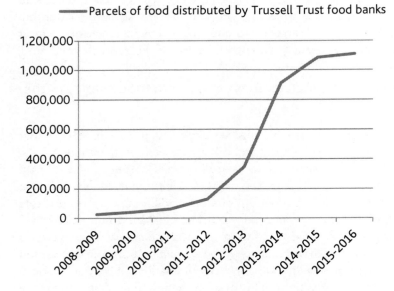

— Parcels of food distributed by Trussell Trust food banks

Trussell Trust Foodbank Network had 445 projects, which distributed 1,084,604 parcels of food (Trussell Trust, n.d.a).

The number of food banks also rose in these years – from 132 food banks in 2010–11, to 345 in 2012–13, to 424 in 2015–16 (Trussell Trust 2011, 2013a, 2016). There has also been an increasing geographical spread. Loopstra et al. (2015) found that, in 2009–10, Trussell Trust food banks were operating within just 29 local authorities; by 2013–14, they operated in 251.

Emergency food provision terminology

A particular terminology is emerging in the UK to describe this new-look food charity and other types of food assistance. The term 'food aid' is increasingly being used by policy makers and non-governmental organisations (NGOs) (Cooper and Dumpleton, 2013; Hansard, 2013). The Department for the Environment, Food and Rural Affairs (Defra) uses the term 'food aid' to encompass a range of different types of short-term assistance with food, and define it as: 'an umbrella term encompassing a range of large-scale and small local activities aiming to help people meet food needs, often on a short-term basis during crisis or immediate difficulty; more broadly they contribute to relieving symptoms of household or individual level food poverty and poverty' (Lambie-Mumford et al., 2014, p.iv). Within this broader category, both state (for example, welfare food vouchers) and non-state support are situated. Non-state-provided support in the form of charitable initiatives is of particular interest for this book – especially charitable emergency food assistance. While such assistance includes a whole range of initiatives, such as hot meal providers or soup runs, 'food banks' have dominated the discourse and debate in the UK in recent years.

Food banks

Food banks have come to be recognised as charitable initiatives that provide emergency parcels of food for people to take away, prepare and eat (Lambie-Mumford and Dowler, 2014). This provision is usually given to help relieve some kind of food crisis. While this food-bank label is quite high profile and dominates the food charity debate, it belies significant variability among the projects that identify themselves as such – including differences in the food provided, how the food banks are accessed, when they are open and if other services are on offer at the project (Dowler and Lambie-Mumford, 2015). Overall, the sheer range in type and size of the wider charitable emergency food provision category makes their full extent and coverage hard for policy makers and researchers to capture.

International understanding of 'food banks'

Importantly, terminology around emergency food provision can vary between countries. For example, in the US and many European countries, the term 'food bank' usually refers to warehouses or centres that collect, store and redistribute food to charitable organisations, which then pass on the food directly to beneficiaries (Berner and O'Brien, 2004; Costello, 2007; Pérez de Armiño, 2014). In this model, food banks effectively work as 'middle men', collecting and redistributing food but are not themselves client-facing. The food is distributed to charitable organisations – either 'emergency' or 'non-emergency' food programmes (Mabli et al., 2010). Emergency providers include food pantries, soup kitchens and emergency shelters (Berner and O'Brien, 2004; Mabli et al., 2010). Food pantries distribute food for people to take home and prepare themselves (Berner and O'Brien, 2004; Mabli et al., 2010). Soup kitchens provide prepared meals, which are served onsite; emergency shelters provide both shelter and prepared meals to clients in need (Mabli et al., 2010). 'Non-emergency' programmes include, for example, day care centres or summer holiday camps (Mabli et al., 2010).

The discourse in the Canadian context incorporates a broader notion of community-based charitable food assistance, in contrast to the rather more prescribed vocabulary of the US (possibly a result of the influence of models of large-scale national initiatives, such as Feeding America). In Canada, the food-bank model varies and includes initiatives that give food to people directly (Riches, 2002; Tarasuk and Eakin, 2003). Published research also includes work relating to community kitchens, where groups of people 'pool their resources to cook large quantities of food' (Engler-Stringer and Berenbaum, 2007). International aspects are key to this book, so appreciating where definitions converge and diverge is particularly important.

Food banks versus surplus food redistribution

Surplus food redistribution is not usually part of the 'food bank' category in the UK. While some food banks might obtain food for provision from these surplus food redistribution initiatives, unlike in some other countries, these redistributors are not themselves generally recognised as 'food banks'. Arguably, the most important distinction in the UK for the food-bank label is that the projects within it are direct providers to people in need – not providers to community projects that hand out food. There are, however, exceptions to this general rule, which call themselves food banks and look more like European or North American models of these projects – collecting and storing food and distributing it to organisations that provide it to people in need. The Oxford Food Bank (http://oxfordfoodbank.org) is an example of one of these projects.

The two case study organisations for the research on which this book is based – the Trussell Trust Foodbank Network and FareShare – are examples of 'food bank' and 'surplus food redistribution' organisations respectively, and form the biggest national networks of their kind in the UK.

Food charity and food insecurity in other rich countries: what can we learn from international evidence?

The UK is not alone in witnessing the rise of food charity in recent years. The phenomenon has been observed across Europe in the emerging evidence base. Studies on contemporary experiences of food insecurity and food charity have been conducted in Finland (Silvasti and Karjalainen, 2014); Germany (Pfeiffer et al., 2011); Spain (Pérez de Armiño, 2014); Estonia (Kõre, 2014); and France (Rambeloson et al., 2007). In the US and Canada, where food charity has been common for several decades, a well-established evidence base provides further important data on these issues and initiatives (Ahluwalia et al., 1998; Berner and O'Brien, 2004; Bhattarai et al., 2005; Daponte and Bade, 2006; Poppendieck, 1994, 1998; Loopstra and Tarasuk, 2012; Riches, 2002).

The rise of food charity in Europe

In Europe, Germany and Spain have each seen a rise in food banking in recent years. In Germany, 880 food banks fed over one million people in 2011, an increase from 540 food banks in the mid-2000s and 270 food banks in 2000 (Pfeiffer et al., 2011). In Spain, the use of food banks has followed a similar trajectory to Germany and the UK; 700,000 people were helped in 2007, rising to 1.5 million in 2012 (Pérez de Armiño, 2014). As of 2012, half of all congregations or parish unions in Finland delivered food aid, although Silvasti and Karjalainen (2014) situate the origins of this trajectory back to the 1990s. There is, however, a wider and longer history of food banking across Europe;

the European Federation of Food Banks has been in operation since 1986, and has members from 23 European countries (FEBA, n.d.).

Food charity and welfare

As in the UK, the recent rise of food charity in Europe has occurred in the context of increased conditionality and reductions to entitlements in social security. This has happened alongside a delegation of responsibility for caring for those experiencing food insecurity from the state to the charitable sector.

In Germany, the German Social Code II, introduced in 2005, represented a more workfare-oriented social security regime and saw the buying power of payments received reduce significantly (Pfeiffer et al., 2011). In Spain, programmes of austerity since the economic crash of the mid-2000s have had particular impacts on the shape of the welfare state, increasing conditionality, reducing funding for services and contributing to what Pérez de Armiño (2014, p.133) refers to as the Spanish welfare state's 'progressive erosion'.

In Finland, Silvasti and Karjalainen (2014, p.83) argue that a particularly important defining point was the move in the 1990s away from the Nordic model of welfare and towards a more means-tested model, similar to Anglo-Saxon welfare states. Overall, researchers in Germany and Finland have described how these shifts in retrenching welfare states and the concomitant rise in the (food) charity response have amounted to a delegation of responsibility from the state to the charitable sector (Pfeiffer et al., 2011; Silvasti and Karjalainen, 2014).

Importantly, the UK, Spanish, German and Finnish experiences of the growth of food charity in parallel to economic crisis, uncertainty and the retrenchment of the welfare state is similar to other case studies (notably the US, Canada, Australia and New Zealand) in the collection edited by Riches (1997a) in the mid-1990s. In both the US and Canada, the numbers of emergency food projects and people turning to them for help grew in the context of economic recession and reforms to social security that saw reductions in entitlements and a broader programme of welfare retrenchment (Poppendieck, 1998; Riches, 2002).

The efficacy of food charity

The international evidence base – particularly from the North American context – can shed light on the effectiveness of food charity and the key drivers of food charity usage. What this body of work tells us is that food charity systems are vulnerable; precarious; nutritionally inadequate; inaccessible; and not accessed by all of those in need. Ultimately, previous food security analyses have found that emergency food assistance can only provide relief from the *symptoms* of food insecurity, not address the root *causes* of that insecurity (Lambie-Mumford et al., 2014).

Food charity systems provide ad hoc and uncoordinated provision; they have limited resources at their disposal, rely on donated food (from private individuals or corporate partners) and volunteers to run the service and are thus exposed to donor and volunteer fatigue, as well as running out of food (Riches, 1997c, p.173; Silvasti and Riches, 2014, p.203). These systems are highly vulnerable and precarious due to their structures and can offer little guaranteed coverage. A further problem identified in the literature with this provision is that these systems are 'not designed' to meet dietary or nutritional requirements, and do not necessarily provide culturally appropriate foods (Riches, 1997c, p.173; Silvasti and Riches, 2014, p.203).

Given the ad hoc and uncoordinated nature of food charity provision, geographical access and availability can vary significantly and other factors also reduce the accessibility of this provision, including unclear or vague eligibility criteria (Silvasti and Riches, 2014). While the profile and narrative surrounding food charity can imply that this provision is available to and accessed by those in need, research tells us that this is not the case. Evidence indicates that the most food-insecure households are more likely to seek out external help such as emergency food aid, and that the likelihood of food charity usage increases with severity of food insecurity (Bhattarai et al., 2005; Loopstra and Tarasuk, 2012). However, the literature shows that – even in countries where food charity systems are widely established and extensive – uptake among food-insecure households remains relatively low. Yu et al. (2010), for instance, showed that in the US only around one in five food-insecure households sought and received 'informal food support' – findings echoed by Loopstra and Tarasuk (2012), who showed that, in a survey of 371 low-income families in Toronto, 75% were judged 'food insecure', yet only 23% had used a food bank.

Research does tell us there are numerous barriers to accessing food charity. Reasons for people not taking up food charity include a lack of access; insufficient information, different perceptions of food aid (who it is for and what it will provide) or household need (feeling that one is not in extreme need) and negative emotional experiences of indignity and stress (Ahluwalia et al., 1998; Engler-Stringer and Berenbaum, 2007; Loopstra and Tarasuk, 2012).

Strategy of last resort

This body of research on food charity also tells us that individuals and families turn to emergency food provision as a last resort. Households employ a range of strategies for trying to manage limitations to their food access, including drawing on social networks to borrow money or food, eating less varied diets or staggering the payment of bills to release money for food, among many other practices (Ahluwalia et al., 1998; Nnakwe, 2008). Furthermore, asking for emergency food aid from a food charity is not only a strategy of last resort for individuals and households (Ahluwalia et al., 1998; Loopstra and Tarasuk, 2012) but also one of many strategies employed. The evidence suggests that when households do turn to charitable food assistance, they are also likely to be drawing on multiple forms of food and other welfare support, where these exist (Berner and O'Brien, 2004).

Depoliticising effect of food charity

The work of Riches (1997a, among many) is critical for exploring the notion that food charity also serves to depoliticise the issue of household food insecurity and thereby move discussions away from responses that address the root causes of these experiences. The key challenge here is that food charities can 'allow us to believe the problem is being met and they deflect attention away from government and its legislated responsibilities' (Riches, 1997c, p.173); they can also be part of the construction of the issue in the public consciousness as a responsibility for charity rather than policy makers.

The evidence base from other 'rich' countries in the Global North therefore highlights the ineffectiveness of food charity for addressing food insecurity. However, as Silvasti and Riches (2014, p.203) argue, this ineffectiveness is 'hidden by a growing degree of public legitimacy promoted by positive mass media attention'.

Food insecurity definition and measurement

Defining food insecurity

Given that the aim of food charity is to relieve symptoms of household- or individual-level food insecurity, any discussion of its rise must be closely tied to discussions of household- or individual-level food insecurity more generally. A key problem in exploring and arriving at a better understanding of limited access to food in the UK is the fact that terminology and conceptualisation are not well established or widely understood.

In its opening paragraphs, the final report of the Parliamentary Inquiry into Hunger and Food Poverty acknowledges the lack of precision around the problem at hand, but then claims that spending time on better understanding it conceptually 'would not match the urgency that we feel over a number of our fellow citizens going hungry' (Food Poverty Inquiry, 2014b). Before the report, the terms of reference of the Inquiry used the terms 'hunger', 'food poverty' and 'household food security' without corresponding definitions or authoritative use of one particular term over the others (Food Poverty Inquiry, 2014a). These publications are symptomatic of an overall lack of an agreed definition of this experience in the UK.

While the phrase 'food poverty' has popular resonance (Cooper and Dumpleton, 2013; Oxfam, 2013) and a history of utilisation in academic research (Dowler et al., 2001), 'food insecurity' is used by government (Defra, 2006) and by researchers from other countries in the Global North (Loopstra and Tarasuk, 2013; Riches, 1997b). 'Food poverty' and 'food insecurity' have also been used interchangeably in the UK (Dowler and O'Connor, 2012).

Such differing terminology can cause confusion, but what this vocabulary has in common is reference to how well people are able to eat and participate in the socially accepted food culture within the means available to them. The definition of food security offered by Anderson (1990, p.1560) in a report to the American Institute of Nutrition is utilised here:

> access by all people at all times to enough food for an active, healthy life and includes at a minimum: a) the ready availability of nutritionally adequate and safe foods, and b) the assured ability to acquire acceptable foods in socially acceptable ways (for example, without resorting to emergency food supplies, scavenging, stealing and other coping strategies). Food insecurity exists whenever the availability of nutritionally adequate and safe foods or the ability to acquire acceptable foods in socially acceptable ways is limited or uncertain.

According to this definition, food insecurity therefore refers to the problem of having insufficient access to a socially acceptable food experience – something much more than just diet, and with social acceptability at its core. Research in this area also places particular emphasis on social participation through food and the importance of, for example, being able to invite friends or family around for a meal once in a while or being able to have a child's friend over for tea (Lambie-Mumford, 2015).

By way of establishing these experiences in relation to famines, starvation and malnutrition in the Global South, food insecurity and food poverty in richer countries are conceptualised as relative – in a similar way to relative theories of poverty, where 'people's experience of hunger and poverty is directly related to the societies in which they live and the standards of living which are customarily enjoyed' (Riches, 1997b, p.65).

Food insecurity in the UK today

The causes and drivers of household food insecurity remain contested and the academic literature looks at a range of areas – including, for example, food skills and growing. However, of particular relevance to questions of contemporary food insecurity are studies that highlight the role of socioeconomic structures in driving experiences of food insecurity – particularly in relation to economic security; for example, costs of living, income levels and income security (Coleman-Jensen, 2011; De Marco and Thorburn, 2009; Kirkpatrick and Tarasuk, 2011). Findings of these research studies are important in the current context, given the ways in which post-crisis economics (recession and economic uncertainty) and public policies (public finance austerity and welfare reform) are impacting directly on these structural determinants of food insecurity (Dowler and Lambie-Mumford, 2015). The rise of insecure work (such as so-called 'zero-hour contracts'), low-paid work and welfare reform (which has reduced social security entitlements and increased conditionality) are all factors referenced in recent debates about food banks and rising need in the UK (Food Poverty Inquiry, 2014b).

When looking at structural determinants of food insecurity and how they have changed over time (especially income levels, income security, food prices and transport costs), evidence suggests that circumstances have worsened, particularly in the last few years (Hirsch, 2013). Relative to wages and social security levels, prices (including of housing, food and fuel) have risen and access to services and other forms of publicly funded support have been restricted as a result of public finance austerity. Together with evidence suggesting that, when under financial pressure, households cut back on food budgets (perceived to be the most flexible element of household spending, see Dowler, 1997;

Goode, 2012; Hossain et al., 2011), this means that the nature of food insecurity is likely to have changed for the worse over recent years.

Statistics produced by Defra (2014, p.20) show that falling income and rising costs of living resulted in food being over 20% less affordable for those living in the lowest income decile in 2014 compared to in 2003. Recent work by Hossain et al. (2011, p.5) highlights that, during the recession, households were shopping and cooking differently to reduce expenditure, and increasingly relying on social networks for support. A survey commissioned by the national housing charity Shelter (2013) found that, in the year leading up to the survey, 31% of its 4,000 respondents had cut back on food to meet housing costs.

Minimum Income Standards (MIS) research is also particularly helpful here, and highlights the issue of current income inadequacies in terms of minimum wages and benefit levels in particular (Davis et al., 2014; Padley and Hirsch, 2014). According to Padley and Hirsch (2014, p.4), the recession has 'created additional hardship'– especially for young people, single people and those living in privately rented accommodation. In 2012, a report by Save the Children (2012, p.4) found that 60.8% of families surveyed were cutting back on how much they spent on food, 39.1% were eating less fruit and vegetables and 25.5% were serving smaller portions.

When we look at the nature of income crises leading to food-bank use, it appears that there has also been an increase in vulnerability to these shocks in the last few years. Impacts of reduced or insecure incomes and problems associated with social security appear to be leaving increasing numbers of people without income, or with a reduced level of income, leading to food-bank uptake (Lambie-Mumford, 2014; Lambie-Mumford and Dowler, 2014). In particular, delays in benefit payments and sanctions, leaving people without incomes, are key triggers of food-bank use (Perry et al., 2014).

This body of evidence indicates that food insecurity has worsened over the so-called 'age of austerity', with lagging incomes relative to other costs of living forcing households to cut back or trade down on the food they purchase and eat. Moreover, the situation appears to have worsened across the scale of severity; acute experiences of food insecurity – induced by income crises – have increased, particularly in the context of welfare reform.

Measuring food insecurity

In addition to a lack of agreed definition, in the UK there is also a lack of a systematic measurement of food insecurity. While research on 'food poverty' – often used as a synonym of 'food insecurity' (Dowler and O'Connor, 2012) – reaches back decades in the UK (Caraher et al., 1998; Dowler, 1997), household food insecurity is not itself systematically measured.

The Food and Agriculture Organisation recently estimated that 8.4 million people in the UK are experiencing food insecurity (FAO, 2016). While these findings provide important insights, as Taylor and Loopstra (2016) discuss, they are limited in what they can tell us in relation to the household characteristics associated with vulnerability to food insecurity.

Unlike in other countries – including the US and Canada, where regular measures of household food insecurity take place using an established methodology (Coleman-Jensen et al., 2014; Loopstra and Tarasuk, 2013) – the UK does not measure household food insecurity directly (see discussion in Lambie-Mumford and Dowler, 2015). This means that researchers, policy makers and activists in the field of food insecurity have to turn to food-related measures in poverty surveys or proxy indicators; for example, consensual measures of poverty that include indicators of food access (Gordon and Pantazis, 1997; Mack, 1985; Pantazis et al., 2006).

In the absence of available statistics relating to levels of hunger, the numbers of people accessing food banks are increasingly being used as a proxy measure. This is problematic for several reasons: these numbers only account for those visiting projects, not those in equal need who did not or could not access such provision; and a cumulative figure cannot account for repeat visits, so cannot show how many individuals were helped or the extent of unmet need where the number of visits to a single provider is limited (see Lambie-Mumford and Dowler, 2014). Moreover, where need is defined as 'crisis' or 'acute' food insecurity, food-bank statistics do not take account of people experiencing less severe but potentially chronic food insecurity; as such, they can detract attention from the broader structural determinants of these experiences, inhibiting more preventative-focused responses.

But what hunger measures would be and the validity of different methods of measurement remains open for discussion, and requires further detailed debate. Within the context of the global debate on how best to measure hunger – including the merits of objective nutrient-based measures versus more subjective experience-based measures (Webb et al., 2006) – some countries in the Global North have adopted measures of food insecurity that capture the subjective lived experience of hunger (Bickel et al., 2000). Capturing the subjective aspects of the food insecurity experience would be particularly important for a UK-based measure, as this provides a richer understanding of the experience and its specific determinants.

Significance of the lack of food security definition and measurement

Without embracing a conceptualisation and subsequent definition of food insecurity that clearly enables the identification of drivers and determinants – and therefore possibilities for cross-government policy interventions – the issue will continue to be seen as one for markets and policies related to shoring up imports and food supply.

Despite recent calls, ministers have so far rejected the introduction of direct measures in favour of pre-existing proxy monitoring (Hansard, 2016). The lack of measurement means there is no accurate or clear idea of how many people are experiencing food insecurity now or who may be vulnerable to it in the future, making effective preventative and protective responses difficult to identify. Both defining and measuring the food insecurity policy problem will be critical to establishing a policy framework that facilitates effective interventions. The lack of robust definition and measurement is likely to hinder effective policy ownership and action.

International comparative research

While international research can provide important markers for research here in the UK, and indicate where similarities and differences may lie, there are critical challenges facing international comparative research in the areas of both household food insecurity and food charity. These relate again to a lack of consistent conceptualisations and definitions of food insecurity and food charity across countries, and the lack of systematic measurement of food insecurity and food charity provision and use (Lambie-Mumford and Dowler, 2015).

In terms of consistent conceptualisations and definitions in different countries, despite the internationally recognised concept and definition of (household) food insecurity (FAO, 2006) varying conceptualisations and terminology are used in the literature under study. In North America, household food insecurity is most frequently used (Coleman-Jensen et al., 2014; Daponte et al., 2004; Tarasuk, 2001), but elsewhere this terminology can vary – as discussed above in the UK, 'food poverty' is a popular term to describe similar experiences and is used both instead of and as a synonym for food insecurity (Cooper and Dumpleton, 2013; Dowler and O'Connor, 2012; Oxfam, 2013), whereas in Germany the concept 'alimentary participation' is used, which emphasises the social function of food (Feichtinger, 1997; Pfeiffer et al., 2011, 2015).

There is also a lack of consistency in public understanding and academic writings of what different food charity terminology refers to – particularly the term 'food bank'. This term is used to refer to a range of initiatives across countries, including projects that provide food directly and those that store food and send it to charities and other organisations for distribution.

The lack of measurement of food insecurity is a particularly troubling barrier to comparative research. While some countries – notably the US and Canada – do measure household food insecurity levels routinely (Coleman-Jensen et al., 2014; Health Canada, n.d.), other countries conduct no formal monitoring. This is the case in the UK, Germany (Pfeiffer et al., 2011), Spain (Pérez de Armiño, 2014) and elsewhere (Silvasti and Riches, 2014, p.193).

In many countries, there is also a lack of systematic data on charitable food systems – including their structures, coverage of provision, how they are used and by whom. What exists currently in many countries is data collected by food charities or networks of food charities; this is neither systematic nor intended for use and interrogation by policy makers or researchers (see examples in Germany (Pfeiffer et al., 2011), the UK (Lambie-Mumford et al., 2014) and Spain (Pérez de Armiño, 2014)).

UK food charity and household food security policy context

As the nature and extent of food insecurity and food charity changes in the UK, the question of the role of policy becomes more urgent. As food insecurity has risen in visibility, there has been a considerable level of political reaction in the form of parliamentary debates, comments to the media and – most significantly – a Parliamentary Inquiry (Food Poverty Inquiry, 2014b; Hansard, 2013; Wallop, 2009). But as yet there has been little tangible policy response in the shape of targeted interventions or strategies.

Policy void

This policy void occurs in the context of a general lack of policy ownership of the issue of food insecurity. Traditionally in the UK, approaches to ensuring everyone has access to healthy food have been left to the operation of efficient markets in retail and employment, appropriate consumer choice and a social welfare system meant to enable those lacking employment and those unable to work to purchase food (Dowler et al., 2011). However, the evidence of rising food insecurity and increasing numbers of people turning to charitable food sources questions the efficacy of these mechanisms in protecting people from hunger – and, moreover, suggests that they may have ultimately failed. However, this absence of national-level policy response may also in part be explained by the general lack of evidence on the nature of the phenomenon and the particular drivers of need.

Missed policy connections

Responsibility for household-level 'food security' is currently situated within the remit of Defra (2006). However, policy makers in the UK have only relatively recently applied the notion of food security to the household level with limited indicators developed in the late 2000s (MacMillan and Dowler, 2011). While the issue of household access to food is formally located within Defra's remit, it nonetheless intersects with areas of responsibility in other Whitehall departments, therefore opening up the possibility of cross-Whitehall commitment and working. For example, food insecurity relates to the work of the Department for Work and Pensions (DWP) on social security levels and tax credits; the Department of Health's (DoH) work on the consequences of poor diet on health; and community access to adequate shops as part of the Department for Communities and Local Government's role in planning guidelines. Despite these intersections, there has been little formal engagement with developing cross-governmental approaches to addressing the structural root causes of food insecurity to date.

Recent political reactions and responses to food banks

The growth of food banks has been and continues to be an increasingly high-profile issue, and has sparked reaction from all sectors – including NGOs, the media and private and public sectors. There has also been considerable political reaction from politicians at local, devolved and national levels (for example, see Hansard, 2013). Used by some as representative of a failing welfare state and others as representative of community responsiveness, these have so far remained rhetorical reactions and have yet to translate into substantive policy responses driven by elected members of councils, assemblies or parliament. At the national level, there has so far been no policy response from policy makers within the aforementioned government departments. While officers in devolved and local governments have worked on various initiatives, such as grant funding or food strategies, these have been local and often short- or medium-term responses (Dowler and Lambie-Mumford, 2015). In the absence of a state response to rising need, charitable food initiatives (such as food banks and initiatives to which FareShare distributes food) continue to be left to respond as best they can to the needs they face in their local communities.

Promising policy interjections

There have, however, been several notable interjections in the policy debate. 2014 saw the publication of a flagship report by a collaboration of some of the UK's most high-profile poverty NGOs (Perry et al., 2014) and the report resulting from the Parliamentary Inquiry into Hunger and Food Poverty (Food Poverty Inquiry, 2014b, 2014c). These reports were groundbreaking in three ways.

First, they provided a unique amount of evidence into the under-researched field of hunger in the UK. The *Emergency use only* (Perry et al., 2014) report drew on data from over 1,100 food-bank clients, and the Parliamentary Inquiry received over 400 pieces of oral and written evidence (Food Poverty Inquiry, 2014b). These reports thus represented a significant step forward in our knowledge about hunger and food-bank use.

Second, they symbolised a public acknowledgement of the will to address the issue of hunger. The rise of food banks has been a contested and politically heated issue ever since the phenomenon rose to prominence a few years ago, and these reports clarify the commitment of key stakeholders in the voluntary and community sector – as well as, for the first time, in government – to work towards a 'zero-hunger Britain' (Food Poverty Inquiry, 2014b, p.16).

Third, these reports outlined actionable recommendations designed to reduce the need for emergency help to obtain food from projects such as food banks. These include particularly important suggestions around raising incomes and enabling a more effective social security system. The parliamentary report outlines recommendations that seek both long- and short-term change. It contains numerous measures (approximately 19 out of a total of 77) that aim to facilitate socioeconomic shifts in wage levels and costs of living (particularly food, fuel and housing), designed to enable people to afford food and other essential costs. Both the parliamentary and *Emergency use only* reports also dedicate a significant proportion of their recommendations to the social security system. These recommendations are detailed and relate to ways in which continuity of income can be promoted and provision (particularly crisis provision) strengthened.

Later, in 2015, the Fabian Society published the report from their commission on Food and Poverty (Tait, 2015). This report called for government to take direct responsibility for household food insecurity in the UK; it set out guiding principles and particular points for 'strong government-coordinated action' (p.1). Together, these three interjections provide a promising start for the development of effective policy responses to household food insecurity.

Outlining the policy problem

Yet what is lacking overall in this body of analysis and prescription is clarity over the exact nature of the overarching policy problem and the specific ways in which these recommendations would address it. While a rush to action brought about by a moral imperative is understandable, it must also be realised that, if the policy problem is not clearly articulated, effective policy responses could well be hindered.

Employing agreed concepts in policy – such as household food insecurity – has several key benefits. First, it highlights different layers within these experiences – notably chronic and acute experiences – both of which require distinct responses. Second, it enables structural determinants and possible points for policy intervention to be identified. Just as importantly, however, clearer articulations of the policy problem at hand will also facilitate a better understanding of what the problem is *not*. A handful of recommendations from the Parliamentary Inquiry refer to levels of food waste and the role redistribution could play in supplying charitable provision. Food waste and food insecurity are both undeniably symptoms of dysfunctional food and socioeconomic systems – but they are distinct policy problems, and should not be conflated. Certainly, one (food waste) should not be seen as a way to overcome the other (food insecurity).

Other recommendations of the Parliamentary Inquiry concerning emergency food provision – and indeed the very title of the Inquiry report itself (*Feeding Britain*) – also imply that the best response to acute experiences lies in further embedding charitable emergency food provision. Again, although these initiatives are important sites of care and solidarity in local communities, the concept of 'food insecurity' actually works to highlight the fact that the determinants of acute experiences (and therefore their prevention and alleviation) lie elsewhere: with core questions of adequate income and effective social security.

All three of the major reports published provide important recommendations for action that would help to address acute and chronic experiences of food insecurity, including raising wages and improving the social security system. They do move the debate forward. That said, focus still needs to be placed on the large sections of these reports that highlight the need to reevaluate the adequacy and efficacy of the whole of the UK's social security system and the wider political-economic structures within which the system is embedded. At root, it is these structures that influence people's standards of living – and, ultimately, their ability to feed themselves and their families.

One of the most pressing challenges to adequate policy responses is the aforementioned lack of monitoring of, and robust evidence on, drivers of food insecurity and intersections between food insecurity and food-bank use. Without a proper understanding of the scale of food insecurity and its drivers (that is, possible points for policy interventions), adequate policy responses will be hard to identify and evidence.

Food and social policy

In practice what we have seen develop in the UK in terms of policy responses to low-income households' access to food is an emphasis on social security payments, which are meant to cover living costs (including food) in the main, supplemented by specific programmes targeted at particular groups in the population, notably children and pregnant women; importantly, however, these are top-up provisions to social security payments or low wages.

The foundations of the welfare state in the UK were built upon Beveridge's five giants of 'want, squalor, idleness, ignorance and disease' (Beveridge, 1942). However, Dowler has argued that, in constructing the welfare state, issues of food availability and accessibility were 'largely bypassed' (Dowler, 2003, p.140) and interventions are either premised in welfare support (social security) or development of human capital (mothers and children) (Dowler et al., 2001). Historically, UK social policy research has addressed hunger as just one element (albeit an important one) in the definition, measurement and lived experience of poverty. Having the resources to access a customary diet was at the forefront of Townsend's (1979, p.31) definition of poverty, and questions relating to the types of diet and food experiences (such as being able to invite friends or family over for a meal) are established measures in surveys such as Breadline Britain and the Poverty and Social Exclusion Survey (Gordon and Pantazis, 1997; Gordon et al., 2000; PSE, 2012). Importantly, these surveys measure food experiences as much more than minimum diet and nutritional intake. They incorporate the facilitative social dynamics embodied in food experiences, such as sharing food with others, reciprocating food-based activities and eating similarly to others – in other words, being able to take an active part in a socially embedded food culture.

Food and social security

The approach adopted in the UK contrasts to social policy programmes in other countries – most notably the US, where food voucher schemes are much more prominent parts of the welfare safety net. Poppendieck (2014, p.176) reports on the extent of food provision through the 'big five' food programmes in the US: one in seven Americans are enrolled on the Supplemental Nutrition Assistance Programme; the National School Lunch Programme and School Breakfast Programme together serve 7.5 billion meals a year; 9 million pregnant women, infants and preschool-aged children are enrolled on the Special Supplemental Nutrition Programme for Women, Infants and Children; and nearly 3.5 million people receive meals through the Child and Adult Care Feeding Programme.

While social policy responses to the accessibility of food in the context of low income and poverty rely on social security payments as the main source of support, work on MIS shows significant gaps between what social security provides and the income that minimum standards of living require. As of 2015, out-of-work benefit incomes provide 40% of the income required to obtain a minimum standard of living for a single working-age adult, and 57% for a couple with two children and one parent with one child (Hirsch, 2015b). Importantly, this proportion has reduced in recent years –particularly for families with children, for whom these payments used to provide around two thirds of MIS (Hirsch, 2015a).

Healthy Start and free school meals

Outside of these social security payments are other initiatives designed to facilitate better access to food, which are managed by other government departments. While DWP oversees out-of-work benefit programmes, the DoH manages the Healthy Start food voucher scheme and the Department for Education and individual local authorities manage school meal and snack programmes. The Healthy Start Scheme replaced the Welfare Food Scheme in 2006, and provides vouchers (for formula and cow's milk and fresh or frozen fruit and vegetables) to pregnant women and children under the age of four (Lucas et al., 2015). Families are eligible if their income is below £16,190 a year, they are in receipt of tax credits or out-of-work benefits or the mother is aged under 18. The vouchers are worth £3.10 each. The scheme provides two vouchers per week for each child under 12 months, and one voucher per week per pregnant woman and child aged 12–48 months (Lucas et al., 2015).

Parents of school-aged children do not have to pay for school meals if they are in receipt of income support or out-of-work benefits, tax credits or state pension credit (Long, 2015). From September 2014, free school meals were made universal for all children in reception class and school years one and two (5–7 years old) (Long, 2015). The School Fruit and Vegetable Scheme, established after the publication of the National Health Service plan in 2000, is also available to promote access to healthy foods for children; it provides one portion of fruit or vegetables every day to all children aged 4–6 years old in state-funded schools (NHS, 2015). The 2013 School Food Plan announced £3.15 million for breakfast club provision in schools with a 40% or higher free school meal entitlement (Dimbleby and Vincent, 2013). This approximately £6 million (including match funding by the successful tenderers) investment was designed to set up breakfast clubs in 500 schools over 2 years (Dimbleby and Vincent, 2013).

Food charity and the changing welfare state

Contextualising the 'era of austerity'

The growth of emergency food provision – since the turn of the century, but particularly in the last 7 years – has occurred in parallel with significant changes to the welfare state. Since the economic crash in the mid-2000s, the UK has seen a programme of extensive cuts to services that form part of the welfare state, and widespread reforms to social security – what some have termed an 'age of welfare austerity' (Farnsworth, 2011, p.251).

As a defining 'era' of welfare state development, 2010 marked the end of 13 years of New Labour governments and the arrival of a Conservative-led Coalition government (in coalition with the Liberal Democrat Party). Coming into government in the wake of the economic crash and in the middle of a recession, the government introduced stringent austerity measures – including some of the largest cuts to public finance ever seen and some of the most extensive welfare reforms since the introduction of the welfare state in the 1940s (Beatty and Fothergill, 2013; Taylor-Gooby and Stoker, 2011). This fits into a wider historical trajectory of neoliberal shifts in the shape and nature of the welfare state since the 1970s, which involved increasingly individualised notions of risk and care, increased conditionality and communitarian and contractarian interpretations of dependency and solidarity (Dean, 2008; Ellison and Fenger, 2013).

The rise of these particular forms of food charity provides a specific case study of the increasingly prominent role the UK charitable sector is playing in caring for people in or at risk of poverty and food insecurity. Food banks have come to be seen to represent key elements of this reshaped welfare state, with their embedded 'mix of libertarian paternalism and communitarian forms of social solidarity' (Ellison and Fenger, 2013, p.616).

There has also been a discursive shift: alongside the increasing emphasis on individualised notions of responsibility and risk (for poverty), there has been a renewed and increasing emphasis on the notions of 'deserving' and 'undeserving' poor people. As Ellison and Fenger (Ellison and Fenger, 2013, p.616) describe it, there has been a 'proactive demonization and pathologisation of people who are unable or unwilling to participate in the formal labour market'. Political and media discourse pitting 'strivers' and 'hard-working families' against 'welfare scroungers', 'skivers' or 'shirkers' is increasingly common and representative of this shift (Chorley, 2013; Jowitt, 2014; Williams, 2013).

Impact of reforms on food charity

The food-bank response has, to date, been characterised by its charitable nature – it is situated outside of the state. However, the charitable food-bank response has been defined and influenced in important ways by public policy, and particularly what the state provides in terms of poverty prevention and alleviation. Both the contemporary experience of food insecurity and the food-bank response are results of wider shifts in social policy in recent decades (especially since the mid-2000s) and the changing nature of the welfare state – particularly changes in what the state provides in welfare (through services and social security) and the changing role and shape of the voluntary and community sector.

The contemporary era of austerity and welfare reform therefore raises two particularly important issues when considering the growth of emergency food provision in the UK. First, how are these dynamics driving need for food banks and other forms of emergency food provision (particularly in the case of public finance austerity and social security reform)? Second, how are they shaping the nature of the food charity response (particularly in relation to Big Society policies and recent shifts in the shape and role of the voluntary sector paving the way for highly professionalised national-scale organisations)?

Reforms driving the need for food charity

Reforms to welfare processes and entitlements have affected the need for food banks in several ways, as this book (particularly Chapter Seven) will demonstrate (Lambie-Mumford, 2014; Lambie-Mumford and Dowler, 2014; Perry et al., 2014). Changes to levels of entitlements – such as capping benefit income and introducing conditions on the size of housing for which people can claim support (often referred to as the 'bedroom tax') – have reduced incomes overall. Simultaneously and significantly, though, processes including benefit sanctions and administrative delays in payments are leaving people without any income at all – factors that have been identified as key triggers to food-bank use (Perry et al., 2014). Public spending cuts to services are also associated with the need for food banks. Cuts elsewhere mean that practitioners were referring people to food banks where before they may have had discretionary funds for social assistance – for example, cash to buy food or fuel (Lambie, 2011; Lambie-Mumford, 2013).

Reforms shaping the nature of food charity

Other factors in the changing welfare state have also influenced the nature of the response in the form of charitable food banks. The New Labour years were particularly important for the changing role of the voluntary sector. They saw the increased role of the voluntary sector in welfare services through programmes of diversification, and consequently a more formalised and professionalised voluntary sector generally. In the context of the Coalition government (2010–15), this process of diversification continued under the policy platform of the 'Big Society' – based on an ideology of localism and transferring power to individuals and communities (Cabinet Office, 2010). These shifts have resulted in the professionalisation and expansion of the role of the voluntary sector (Alcock, 2010). This has meant that both the nature of voluntary organisations and the expectations that government and society has of them has changed. These organisations are increasingly professional and business-like, and there are increased expectations that they will meet needs in local communities where the state may not. Charitable food provision in the form of the Trussell Trust Foodbank Network is an embodiment of this: operating as a not-for-profit franchise and assuming increasing amounts of responsibility for alleviating hunger in the absence of adequate state-based responses.

What we are seeing, then, is arguably both an organisational phenomenon and a food insecurity phenomenon, with numerous points for social science exploration. Overall, the changing dynamics of hunger and the rise of a charitable response to it appear to be influenced in important ways by wider shifts in social policy. Experiences of hunger are being shaped by the pulling back of state social security, and civil society – in the form of food banks – is increasingly assuming responsibility for responding to crisis needs in the absence of adequate state support.

Note

[1] Whilst 'Foodbank' is the name given to the Trussell Trust network and to individual projects within it; the term 'food bank' is used throughout the book to categorise them as a particular type of emergency food initiative.

THREE

Theories of the food insecurity 'problem' and the right to food 'solution'

This chapter sets out theoretical approaches to both food security and the human right to food. Food insecurity is employed here as a specific way of interpreting the 'problem' that leads people to seek assistance from emergency food providers, and the right to food as a way of envisaging not just the 'solution' to these experiences but a more comprehensive approach to the realisation of socially just food experiences for all. So, while the notion of 'food security' is a prerequisite for the realisation of the right to food, the progressive realisation of this right actually incorporates much more, as will be discussed.

Terminology surrounding food poverty, food insecurity and hunger are not necessarily clearly defined, widely used or understood in the UK. As such, this chapter begins by setting out a clear conceptualisation and definition of the problem of food insecurity. This is informed not only by previous work on food poverty and food insecurity but also by theoretical work on poverty itself, particularly that of Lister (2004). The right to food, its historical context and the UK's relationship to it are also set out.

Two particular aspects of the right to food are focused on: issues of adequacy, acceptability and sustainability; and the state's obligation to respect, protect and fulfil the right. These two elements are explored through utilising several concepts and theories for framing the analysis of empirical data: othering; agency; care; and social protection. By employing these concepts the book engages food insecurity and the right to food with literatures on exclusion, power, care ethics and welfare states.

A theory of food insecurity

The variety of language used to describe the experience of lack of access to food is a significant challenge to UK research in this field. 'Hunger', 'food poverty' and 'food insecurity' are all utilised, and food poverty and insecurity have come to be used interchangeably in the

UK (see Dowler and O'Connor, 2012). The idea of food poverty has particular resonance when applied to household-level experiences (BBC, 2014; Cooper and Dumpleton, 2013; Dowler et al., 2001; Hitchman et al., 2002; Lang et al., 2010; Oxfam, 2013). 'Food security', on the other hand, has often (but not always) been used to refer to national food supply issues and global or national food systems rather than lived household experiences, particularly by the UK government (Kneafsey et al., 2013).

Defining household food insecurity

'Household food insecurity' has been chosen for use in this book for several key reasons. The concept emphasises the social dimensions (adequacy and acceptability) of these experiences; highlights the importance of security into the future; enables us to think in terms of scales of severity; helps to highlight the structural determinants of lack of access to food; and is an internationally recognised concept (thus important for facilitating comparative analysis).

The concept of food insecurity has also been favoured over other concepts, including 'hunger' and 'nutrition insecurity'. Hunger – like malnourishment or nutrition insecurity – is viewed, for the purposes of this research, as tied up with physical biological states. Given the importance of social dynamics and processes to the experiences under study here, such biologically focused conceptualisations do not provide enough theoretical depth.

Conceptualisations and terminology surrounding food insecurity vary and have evolved over time – particularly at an international level, through the work of the Food and Agriculture Organisation (FAO) and others (FAO, 1983, 2006). Researchers have charted the changing nature of food security definitions and the shifts that have occurred, including in relation to scale (from a focus on national and international dimensions to the household and individual levels) and an increasing emphasis on access to and availability of food (Jarosz, 2011; Maxwell, 1996). The definition of food insecurity utilised by the FAO is, despite reference to food preference, still relatively narrow for the purposes of this study: 'Food security exists when all people, at all times, have physical and economic access to sufficient, safe and nutritious food that meets their dietary needs and food preferences for an active and healthy life' (World Food Summit 1996 definition as quoted in FAO, 2006, p.1).

Anderson (1990) offers a more comprehensive definition. This definition is the starting point for much food insecurity research in other countries in the Global North (Coleman-Jensen et al., 2014; Tarasuk, 2001), and is adopted for this book:

> access by all people at all times to enough food for an active, healthy life and includes at a minimum: a) the ready availability of nutritionally adequate and safe foods, and b) the assured ability to acquire acceptable foods in socially acceptable ways (for example, without resorting to emergency food supplies, scavenging, stealing and other coping strategies). Food insecurity exists whenever the availability of nutritionally adequate and safe foods or the ability to acquire acceptable foods in socially acceptable ways is limited or uncertain. (Anderson, 1990, p.1560)

This definition is particularly helpful given the ways in which it emphasises the social dimensions of acceptability and adequacy, which are key themes in both this book and the normative content of the right to food framework. This definition also highlights the importance of security into the future, with emphasis on 'assured ability' to acquire food contrasted against this ability being 'limited or uncertain'. When operationalised, the concept of food security is measured in terms of 'mild, moderate and severe' levels (see for example FAO, 2016 and PROOF, n.d.). This is an important analytical consideration, given that a focus on emergency food provision can sometimes emphasise acute experiences of severe food insecurity over a more comprehensive exploration that also includes mild, moderate and chronic experiences.

Food insecurity, structure and agency

Interpretations of key questions about the nature of the 'problem' are also embedded in this definition – most significantly, whether it is an issue of structure or agency. The interpretation offered in this definition draws on the work of others (Coleman-Jensen, 2011; De Marco and Thorburn, 2009; Kirkpatrick and Tarasuk, 2011), which finds that that food insecurity is an experience determined by structural forces including the food production and retail system; the labour market; the welfare state; transport, housing and planning infrastructures. Income levels and costs of living (including food prices but also housing and energy costs) appear to be particularly important on the basis of contemporary research on food, and poverty and food experiences in the context of the recent recession (see review in Lambie-Mumford et al., 2014).

To emphasise the importance of structure does not, however, 'necessarily write human agency out' (Lister, 2004, p.51). Indeed, there are many ways in which agency can be recognised, valued and accounted for in such interpretations, which are drawn on here. Those experiencing food insecurity can be seen as active agents within this experience. While their agency may be constrained by the structural determinants of their food experiences, notions of 'personal agency' (Lister, 2004) and the ways in which people 'get by' in these circumstances can be accounted for. Such an approach sees the structure/agency issue as: 'people experiencing poverty are actors in their own lives, but within the bounds of frequently formidable and oppressive structural and cultural constraints, which are themselves the product of others' agency' (Lister, 2004, p.157).

Food insecurity or poverty?

One of the key theoretical and empirical tensions embedded throughout this book is the question of whether the 'problem' that emergency food organisations are responding to is one of food insecurity or of poverty. Food insecurity could be said to fit within wider notions of relative poverty and socially defined minimum living standards. However, experiences of food insecurity are seen here as more than a symptom of poverty; they are treated as a site of analysis in their own right, as a set of experiences that both result from and contribute to social exclusion and injustice.

The conceptualisation of food insecurity utilised for this book encapsulates a broad notion of a dynamic process; one that is experienced differently by different people, who have active agency in how they manage their lives within the structural determinants constraining their food experiences. Ultimately, food insecurity is understood as relative to different societies and as a construct of those societies. This conceptualisation has been actioned in this book by Anderson's (1990) aforementioned definition, which takes account of the key composite dynamics of access (broadly defined), acceptability, adequacy and longer-term security. It is a definition that highlights the importance of food for social participation and the value of aspirations and equity.

While the debate on definitions of food insecurity remains open, adopting household food insecurity (as opposed to food poverty in particular) has important benefits when it comes to internationalisation. There are internationally recognised definitions; Anderson's (1990) has formed the basis of much international work, and provides a common conceptual ground on which comparative work might be possible.

Broader theories of poverty can, however, be drawn on to inform the conceptualisation of the food insecurity 'problem', and also to critically engage with the notion of need for emergency food provision in the form of food crisis. The work of Ruth Lister (2004) on the concept of poverty provides a particularly useful way of thinking about conceptualisations, definitions and measurements of related social problems.

Three principles for understanding conceptualisations of the lived experience of food insecurity are drawn here as parallels to conceptualisations of poverty (Lister, 2004). In the first instance, following Riches (1997b), this book sees food insecurity as being, like poverty, a 'construction of specific societies' (Lister, 2004, p.3). It is understood as a relative concept, but one that – like Townsend's (1979, p.31) interpretation of poverty – can be 'defined objectively and applied consistently'.

Food insecurity is also seen as a 'dynamic process rather than a fixed state' (Lister, 2004, p.157) – embodying, as it does, complex interacting processes that operate at every scale (from the global to the interpersonal) and are played out in ever-shifting lived realities.

Finally, the conceptualisation of food insecurity offered here also takes account of the 'multifarious ways in which poverty [or food insecurity] is experienced' (Lister, 2004, p.176). How it is experienced over time; by different people between households and within households; at different life stages; in the context of different tastes, preferences and health circumstances are just a few factors meaning that experiences of food insecurity are lived in different and complex ways. This emphasis on lived experiences also highlights how the experience is lived beyond the individual and family and into wider social interactions. For example being unable to have friends or family around for tea and biscuits, or to send a child to school with a packed lunch similar to their friends'. Here we see the important ways in which food insecurity contributes to experiences of social exclusion.

The capabilities approach

While structural theories of poverty (see Lister, 2004; Townsend, 1979) provide important insights for the conceptualisation of food insecurity, it is useful to explore wider debates surrounding this approach to poverty – particularly those set out by Sen (1983, 1985), given the centrality of his work to the development of human rights theories and the theoretical rights-based framework of this book (Sen, 2004, 2008). In a famous exchange with Townsend (1985), Sen (1983, 1985) set out a thesis for understanding relative and absolute notions of poverty in relation to the concept of 'capabilities'. It could be argued that someone is absolutely deprived – this being distinguished from a notion of relative deprivation in the form of 'commodities, incomes and resources' (Sen, 1983, p.153). 'Poverty, in my view, is not ultimately a matter of incomes at all; it is one of a failure to achieve certain minimum capabilities' (Sen, 1985, p.670). Hick's (2012, p.303) analysis of the capabilities framework argues that this approach 'stresses the intrinsic importance of people's capabilities (as ends) as opposed to the instrumental importance of their incomes (as means)'.

When thinking about food insecurity and its relationship to this particular approach to understanding poverty, the capabilities approach offers a particularly useful tool insofar as it draws attention to all the different possible constraints on people's capabilities – beyond a lack of resources (Hick, 2012). Extending this to the idea of food insecurity, a capabilities approach might then enable us to think not only about income and affording food but also about the physical accessibility of food and other food environments (such as schools). Ultimately, however, the capabilities approach is problematic from the perspective of this research and contrary to many of the other theoretical underpinnings on which the book is based.

In the first instance, the capabilities framework separates 'capabilities' from 'resources' and 'functionings' – yet the theory of food insecurity offered here highlights the importance of the interconnections between these (Dean, 2009; Sen, 1983). Furthermore, the importance of household income could be played down by such a framework, which would be contrary to much of the evidence on the main drivers of food insecurity.

Dean (2009) offers two critiques of the capabilities framework, which are particularly important here. The first is that the capabilities framework does not take sufficient account of structural determinants of poverty (or indeed capabilities). Instead, it abstracts individuals (and notions of their capabilities) from the 'relations of power' within which identity and life chances are constituted (Dean, 2009, p.267) and takes no account of the constraints imposed by capitalist modes of production (Dean, 2009, pp.271–2).

Structural dynamics and the ways in which they construct and constrain people's abilities to achieve minimum standards of living (and food experiences) are critical to the approach to food insecurity adopted in this book. It could also be argued that an explicitly structural framework could – just as much as a capabilities framework – draw attention to, and appropriately emphasise the importance of, the wide array of constraints to food security beyond income. For example, structural framings provide a lens for exploring local food environments, household composition, intrahousehold dynamics and institutional food settings.

The second critique set out by Dean (2009) lies in the liberal nature of the capabilities thesis. The individualistic focus of the capabilities framework sits in contrast to care ethics approaches – also key to the theoretical foundations of this book – which are based on a relational ontology (Dean, 2009, p.268). The importance and contemporary role of social relationships and solidarity are central to this book and to understanding both the nature of food insecurity and the rise of the food charity response. To adopt an individualistic liberal underpinning to experiences of food insecurity would again detract from important dynamics at work, which have been evidenced in previous food insecurity literature; for example, the role of the welfare system, the importance of social networks and how community initiatives respond.

Capabilities and human rights

Sen's capabilities approach has featured prominently in the development of human rights theories. In his paper, Sen (2004) discusses the role of capabilities in helping to enlighten the idea of freedom (of opportunity) within human rights theory. In doing so, however, Sen maintains a focus on shifting emphasis away from means, which is problematic. What is developed in this framework which could be of use here, however, is Sen's (2004, p.334) emphasis on a person being 'free to use this opportunity or not'. He goes on, 'The fact that many of the terrible deprivations in the world seem to arise from a lack of freedom to avoid these deprivations ... is an important motivational reason to emphasise the role of freedom' (Sen, 2004, p.335). Setting aside the insistence that means should be less of a focus than capabilities (but maintaining an emphasis on this particular notion of freedom) strengthens a structural theory of poverty or food insecurity in relation to a human rights approach. It does so by highlighting the importance of how opportunities – in this case, to participate in a socially acceptable food experience – are constrained by external factors, and where opportunities for intervention may lie within those.

Linking food insecurity and the human right to food

Before moving on from food insecurity to explore the right to food in more detail, it is useful to clarify the relationship between the two. Food insecurity is understood here as a conceptualisation and definition of the problem underlying need for emergency food provision. Overcoming this is necessary for realising the right to food – but the human rights approach incorporates more than this notion of equity. Access to a socially acceptable food experience for all (the abolition of food insecurity) is understood in the context of an understanding of food and the human right to food as a social ethic; as a commitment to this right, which in itself is seen as a social good. The right to food is both an aim and an ethic; while the elimination of food insecurity is a prerequisite, it does not (as will be explored next) comprise the whole right to food approach.

The human right to food

The right to adequate food was originally enshrined in Article 25 of the Universal Declaration of Human Rights (ratified in 1948) as part of the right to an adequate standard of living, which incorporated adequate food (United Nations, n.d.). As part of the range of economic, social and cultural rights, the right to food was not ratified by states – including the UK – until the mid-1970s, in the form of the International Covenant on Economic, Social and Cultural Rights (ICESCR) (CESCR, 1999; Joint Committee on Human Rights, 2004; United Nations, 1966). Since then, the UN Economic and Social Council published work on the particularities of the right in 1999, specifically in the form of General Comment 12 on the Right to Adequate Food (CESCR, 1999). There has also been the development of Voluntary Guidelines in support of the realisation of the right to food (FAO, 2005) and, since the mandate was established in 2000, there has been a dedicated UN Special Rapporteur on the Right to Food (OHCHR, n.d.).

General Comment 12, adopted by the UN Committee on Economic, Social and Cultural Rights, outlines some of the 'principal issues' the Committee considers to be important in relation to the 'right to adequate food' (CESCR, 1999). The Committee sees the human right to food as 'of crucial importance for the enjoyment of all rights', and elaborates on both the normative content and obligations and violations of the right (CESCR, 1999). The normative content found in Comment 12 outlines that: 'The right to adequate food is realised when every man, woman and child, alone or in community with others, have physical and economic access at all times to adequate food or means for its procurement' (CESCR, 1999).

Despite close links with the FAO (2006) food security definition, the normative content of the right to food is interpreted as much broader, emphasising the 'adequacy and sustainability of food availability and access'. These are interpreted in specific ways by Comment 12: the precise meaning of 'adequacy' is to a large extent determined by prevailing social, economic, cultural, climatic, ecological and other conditions, while 'sustainability' incorporates the notion of long-term availability and accessibility (CESCR, 1999, p.3). In elaborating further on these two guiding normative principles (in addition to nutrition and food safety-specific content, which are beyond the scope of the book), the normative content of the guidelines emphasises 'cultural or consumer acceptability'; the availability of food; and the physical and economic accessibility of food.

In detailing the obligations and violations the right imposes, Comment 12 outlines that the principal obligation of states 'is to take steps to achieve *progressively* the full realisation of the right to adequate food' (emphasis in original). As with all human rights, the right to food imposes three types of obligations on states – to respect, protect and fulfil the right (CESCR, 1999):

> The obligation to respect existing access to adequate food requires States parties not to take any measures that result in preventing such access.
>
> The obligation to protect requires measures by the State to ensure that enterprises or individuals do not deprive individuals of their access to adequate food.
>
> The obligation to fulfil (facilitate) means the state must proactively engage in activities intended to strengthen people's access to and utilisation of resources and means to ensure their livelihood, including food security. Finally, whenever an individual or group is unable, for reasons beyond their control, to enjoy the right to adequate food by the means at their disposal, States have the obligation to fulfil (provide) that right directly. (CESCR, 1999)

In outlining accountability for the realisation of the right to food, the emphasis is necessarily placed on states, given that they are the actors party to the ICESCR. Having said this, Comment 12 (CESCR, 1999) does make room for the role of people, non-governmental organisations and the private sector in realising the right to adequate food:

> While only States are parties to the Covenant and are thus ultimately accountable for compliance with it, all members of society – individuals, families, local communities, non-governmental organisations, civil society organisations, as well as the private business sector – have responsibilities in the realisation of the right to adequate food. The state should provide an environment that facilitates implementation of these responsibilities. (CESCR, 1999)

Comment 12 (CESCR, 1999) therefore provides an important outline of the detailed content and guiding principles of the right to adequate food. Outlined here by way of an introduction, the normative content and obligations and violations provide the basis of the theoretical framework used to guide the analysis presented in the book (presented in detail later in this chapter).

UK ratification of the right to food

The legal status of the right to food in the UK stems from the ratification of the ICESCR in 1976. This ratification means that the UK government is obliged to respect, protect and fulfil the right to food. The public policy implications of this are far reaching.

In the obligation to *respect* the right to food, the UK government is required not to restrict people's ability to achieve the right to food. The obligation to *fulfil* the right to food also obliges the UK government to take action to identify and implement policies that ensure vulnerable groups of people's access to food. As Ziegler et al. (2011, p.20) state: 'This obligation to fulfil the right to food imposes duties on the state such as the duty to promote distributive taxation and social security. This support should be provided as a matter of right, rather than charity, in order to ensure human dignity.' Finally, the fulfilment of the right to food must be achieved progressively, which means that 'governments must not adopt regressive policies that lead to deterioration in access to food' (Ziegler et al., 2011, p.20). These obligations to respect and fulfil the right to food have particularly important implications for welfare reform and processes such as sanctions – particularly where policy changes are making such provision less accessible, increasingly conditioned and less generous.

In terms of the justiciability of the right to food in the UK, adopting the optional protocol for the ICESCR in 2013 would have been a significant step forward, allowing individuals or groups the chance to bring complaints of violations directly to the CESCR (Ziegler et al., 2011, p.351). However, the UK has failed to ratify this optional protocol, along with the optional protocol to the European Social Charter (Just Fair, 2014; OHCHR, 2014). Despite the lack of progress in these particular areas, there remains hope for the right to food in the UK, which is discussed in more detail in Chapter Eight.

Right to food in an international context

Since 2010, various publications have highlighted the progress that certain other countries have made on the right to food (DeSchutter, 2010; Riches and Silvasti, 2014; Ziegler et al., 2011). Evidence from India, Brazil and South Africa is particularly insightful. Taking the key components set out by DeSchutter (2010) as facilitating progress towards the right to food, examples can be cited for positive developments in relation to the right in state constitutions, justiciability of the right to food in certain countries, the establishment of framework laws and institutional frameworks and national right to food strategies.

The right to food has been incorporated within a number of state constitutions, including both Brazil and South Africa (DeSchutter, 2010; Ziegler et al., 2011). Brazil established framework laws in 2006 (DeSchutter, 2010). Such laws differ depending on the approach taken, and can either provide an umbrella framework or take a more sectoral approach. They might also involve the establishment of monitoring institutions and/or advance the justiciability of the right to food.

Brazil is an example of particularly important institutional frameworks for the right to food. Included within the institutional setup in Brazil is a Special Secretariat for Human Rights, which has within it a Special Commission for Monitoring Violations of the Human Right to Food, a National Rapporteur on the Right to Food, Water and Land and a National Food and Nutritional Security Council (DeSchutter, 2010). The right to food can be operationalised through national right to food strategies, such as that in Brazil – *Frome hunger* (Zero Hunger) – which includes 53 initiatives, overseen at both national and local levels (DeSchutter, 2010).

Examples of the justiciability of the right to food include not only South Africa and Brazil but also India. Ziegler et al. (2011, p.352) argue that India provides 'one of the best examples of the justiciability of the right to food'; in South Africa, economic and social rights have been made justiciable under law. DeSchutter (2010) provides case studies of legal action taken in both Brazil and South Africa, including the class action against the Municipality of Maceió for the violation of the economic, social and cultural rights of families living in the Orla Lagunar Communities and the action taken by traditional fishermen in response to South African legislation that restricted their fishing rights, and therefore their livelihood (DeSchutter, 2010).

Chapter Eight discusses in more detail how these positive developments in other countries could be drawn on to inform and facilitate progressive moves by the UK government towards the realisation of the right to food. Despite the progress made by Brazil and South Africa, however, recent evidence highlights the role still being played by charitable food provision in these countries (Hendricks and McIntyre, 2014; Rocha, 2014). One distinction in Brazil is that public food banks exist there (alongside charitable and corporately run food banks), which are run as government initiatives as part of the *Frome hunger* work (see discussion in Rocha, 2014).

While the application of the right to food to a study of emergency food provision in the UK context is a key innovation of this book, applications to other Global North contexts has a longer history. Riches (1999, 2002, 2011) has long been a proponent of this approach and has written on its implications for Canada. Academics elsewhere are also engaging with what a right to food framework might mean in specific country contexts, including the US (Anderson, 2013; Chilton and Rose, 2009) and the UK and Ireland (Dowler and O'Connor, 2012; Lambie-Mumford, 2013). While there is little recognition and 'considerable resistance' (Dowler and O'Connor, 2012, p.48) to using rights-based frameworks in overcoming poverty and food insecurity in the UK, such a framework offers a clear and comprehensive analytical tool through which to explore the rise and implications of emergency food provision.

Human rights or citizenship rights

Having said this, it is worth exploring why this book focuses on human rights specifically, as opposed to rights based on citizenship. Different approaches to the notion of 'rights' offer distinct ways of understanding the normative underpinnings of those rights, utilise different conceptual tools and ascribe responsibilities in particular ways. Importantly (given the path this book treads between social policy and geographical approaches to the study of food issues), several social policy researchers have noted the different approaches to rights that social policy and human rights researchers have traditionally taken (Dean, 2008; Hosie and Lamb, 2013). Notably, social policy research has tended to focus on the notion of citizens' rights – based on Marshall's (1950) work on social citizenship – which incorporates the notion of welfare rights (see Dean, 2008). This approach is distinct from a human rights approach in several ways.

Normatively, the former approach ties rights to citizenship, where human rights are seen as universal (Hosie and Lamb, 2013). Conceptually, social policy research is often driven by the notion of equity, and – while there is a strong relationship between equality and human rights – human rights incorporates other significant concepts, notably dignity, respect, diversity and autonomy (Hosie and Lamb, 2013). Finally, these divergent approaches to rights are also said to hold different actors responsible. While human rights identify states as 'duty bearers', social policy research is said to eschew this emphasis on the state and to take greater account of other social actors, relationships and structures (Hosie and Lamb, 2013).

In positioning the approach to rights taken in this book, normatively the right to food is seen as a universal (human) right. The notion of such a right being tied to citizenship is seen as problematic, particularly in the context of increasingly mobile populations and the lack of rights ascribed to non-citizens (such as asylum seekers) in these circumstances. Calls for research and emerging evidence relating to destitution within such populations in the UK further problematise this notion when talking about a fundamental right (Crawley et al., 2011). The multitude of conceptual tools the right to food approach provides is also important; this book draws on many of these, emphasising concepts of dignity, acceptability and adequacy. Finally, in terms of notions of responsibility, the book is aligned with the human rights approach to emphasising the role of the state. However, as can be seen in the work of others (such as Sen (2008); also highlighted in CESCR (1999)), a rights approach does take account of the role of actors and structures other than states, government and governance. The approach that human rights takes to attributing responsibility and holding actors to account can therefore more appropriately be articulated in terms of the benefits that human rights approaches could bring when combined with social policy approaches – namely, strengthening arguments for state accountability but simultaneously seeing a wider role for others (Hosie and Lamb, 2013).

Challenges facing the right to food

Putting the right to food approach into practice presents a number of challenges. These include the status of this right as part of a 'second generation' of rights, questions about how effective and attainable rights-based approaches are and tests of feasibility, legality and policy. This section explores these challenges and critically discusses how they might help to formulate clearer and more articulate framings of what the right to food is, and why and how it is appropriate to utilise it in the study of emergency food provision and food insecurity in the Global North.

The right to food is part of the group of so called 'economic, social and cultural rights', which have been referred to as a 'second generation of rights' (behind civil and political rights) (see Dean, 2008). Food formed part of Article 25 of the Universal Declaration of Human Rights, adopted in 1948:

> (1) Everyone has the right to a standard of living adequate for the health and well-being of himself and of his family, including food, clothing, housing and medical care and necessary social services, and the right to security in the event of unemployment, sickness, disability, widowhood, old age or other lack of livelihood in circumstances beyond his control. (United Nations, n.d.)

But it was not until the ICESCR in 1966 (United Nations, 1966) and subsequent guidance (CESCR, 1999) that these rights were explored in further detail. Dean (2008, p.2) refers to these second-generation rights as 'conceptually more abstract and practically more elusive' than first-generation civil and political rights. Herein, arguably, lies the premise of the challenges facing these rights and any research that tries to draw on them; the nature of the obligations placed on signatory states embodies this difficulty. While the ICESCR commits signatory states to the realisation of these rights within the constraints of their available resources (Hosie and Lamb, 2013; United Nations, 1966), 'enforceable duties do not necessarily arise directly or indirectly' (Dean, 2008, p.5).

The abstract and elusive nature of the right to food as an economic, social and cultural right raises questions about the effectiveness and attainability of these rights – an important question to address in the context of social research that seeks progressive opportunities for ways forward. As Lister (2004, p.163) argues: 'While a human rights discourse performs an important symbolic and mobilising function and throws new light on the meaning of poverty, the ultimate test of its effectiveness as a political tool will be the closing of that gap between promise and reality'.

Writing about the human right to health, Sen (2008) sets out some of the key issues that contribute to the sense that such rights are 'remote', and provides thinking around how these can be reconciled in such a way that economic, social and cultural rights can be more effectively articulated and pursued. Sen (2008) sets out three reasons why the right to health may seem remote: the 'legal question' ('how can health be a right since there is no binding legislation demanding just that?'), the 'feasibility question' (that there is 'no way of ensuring that everyone has good health') and the 'policy question' (when the state of people's health is not under the control of policy making) (Sen, 2008, p.2010). Given that what people actually consume and the exact shape of their diets cannot be controlled, there are important parallels between this analysis of the right to health and the right to food. Sen offers solutions to these questions as a way of reconciling these tensions, which form the basis of the interpretation of the right to food used in this book.

The notion of the legal question speaks to a broader issue of understanding the nature of rights. The premise of the question itself assumes that rights are 'inescapably legal' and – drawing on the work of Bentham – are seen as 'a child of the law' (Sen, 2008). Sen argues, however, that rights can be seen differently, as social ethics and ideas of what a good society should have; this in turn enables an interpretation of rights as 'parents' of the law, guiding legislation rather than being derived from it (Sen, 2008).

The question of feasibility can also be countered, according to Sen (2008), with the acceptance of such a right seen as a 'demand to take action to promote that goal'. Therefore, rather than seeing the acceptance of a right as ensuring the right for all, this interpretation sees rights as goals and aspirations. With the question of legislating in the pursuit of a right like health, Sen (2008) argues that it is possible to see a human right as not only a parent of law, 'but also of many other ways of advancing the cause of that right' (p.2010).

Sen's (2008) work can therefore move us beyond critique and towards tangible, practicable ways of both interpreting and putting into action, economic, social and cultural rights. Furthermore, Backman et al.'s (2008) work helps to add nuance to the idea (and critique embedded within the seeming vagueness) of the notion of 'progressive realisation' of rights. While it does not necessarily translate into tangible actions or 'immediate achievement' (The Lancet, 2008) against which states can be held to account, it does require that states improve their performance on human rights 'steadily' (Backman et al., 2008, p.2048). Moreover, the idea that this realisation occurs within the resource constraints experienced by states means that more is required of richer states.

Drawing on these earlier works by Sen (2008) and Backman et al. (2008), it is possible to develop a theoretical approach to understanding the right to food for the purposes of this book. The nature of the right to food as a human right is seen here as a social ethic, and the realisation of this right for all established as a social good. Accepting the right to food is seen as a commitment to this social ethic, translating into a demand to take action to promote this goal. In turn, this commitment can be put into effect when understood as a parent of both laws and actions for the advancement of the right. The call for progressive realisation means that what we should see when this commitment is made and these laws and actions put into place is a continuous, steady, ongoing improvement towards the realisation of the right to food for all – for which the state can be held accountable.

Theoretical framework

The conceptualisations of food insecurity and the right to food outlined earlier form the basis of the theoretical and analytical framework that guides the rest of the book. The right to food in particular, as set out in Comment 12 (CESCR, 1999), not only provides conceptual tools (such as notions of accessibility, adequacy and acceptability) but also draws attention to particular sites for social science investigation around the nature of food acquisition and the roles of different actors in protecting and enabling the right to food. From this, and drawing on key literatures from geographical and social policy research, a specific framework was developed (Figure 2). This section discusses the framework and how it relates to the empirical findings presented in Chapters Four to Seven in particular. The framework has three analytical layers, which guide the book through four empirical chapters.

As articulated in the following section, two key elements outlined in Comment 12 (CESCR, 1999) form the premise of this framework: the normative content relating to the 'adequacy and sustainability of food availability and access'; and the obligations of the state to 'respect, protect and fulfil the human right to food'. The two elements drawn from the right to food give rise to two empirical themes in the book: the normative content surrounding the 'adequacy and sustainability of food availability and access' is framed in relation to the theme of adequacy (Chapters Four and Five), and the notion of obligations is framed in relation to the theme of responsibility (Chapters Six and Seven).

These themes are in turn explored through specific questions regarding the acceptability and sustainability of emergency food systems and the role of charity and the state in realising the right to food. These questions form the basis of four distinct empirical chapters (Chapters Four to Seven), and are answered by utilising the particular concepts and theories of othering, agency, care and social protection.

Figure 2: Theoretical framework

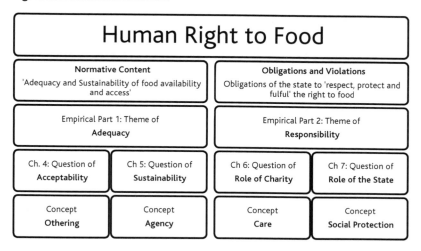

Exploring emergency food provision in relation to normative content of the right to food

The normative content of the right to food, in terms of the adequacy and sustainability of food availability and access, is explored in relation to emergency food provision in a particular way through this analytical framing. 'Adequacy' is taken as the predominant theme; as a lens through which to explore the other embedded aspects of sustainability and access. The overarching theme of adequacy is explored through particular questions relating to the acceptability of emergency food systems as ways of acquiring food (exploring the adequacy of the systems in relation to their social acceptability), and the sustainability of food provided through them and access to that food by those in need (exploring whether access to food through these systems is adequately sustainable).

Acceptability

In the first instance (Chapter Four), the normative content is explored through an initial question of acceptability. Acceptability is taken to be a particularly important concept, given the stipulation in Comment 12 (CESCR, 1999) that the meaning of adequacy relates to specific social, economic and cultural conditions. The idea of 'social acceptability' is particularly relevant, and provides a specific way of interpreting what is meant by 'acceptable' food experiences in a given society. The idea of socially acceptable food experiences relates to the nature of the types of food experiences that prevail in the UK today. This helps to guide an analysis of how acceptable the emergency food provision system is as a method of food acquisition, by drawing attention to how it relates to these prevailing food acquisition methods. The idea of socially acceptable food experiences also relates to the idea of social inclusion as involving participation in these prevailing experiences – being able to shop, cook and eat 'like everyone else'. Exclusion from these socially acceptable mechanisms (including as a result of experiences of food insecurity) is problematic from a right to food perspective. Progressive realisation of the right to food involves full participation in society – and in these socially acceptable food experiences.

To assess the social acceptability of emergency food systems, then, the concept of 'other' is utilised to explore how far these systems constitute acceptable food acquisition methods. Drawing on the work of scholars such as Cloke et al. (2010), Lister (2004) and Midgley (2014), the idea of whether emergency food systems constitute an 'other' system of food acquisition is explored. The concept of 'other' is nuanced and has particular utility in that it enables not only assessments but also degrees of 'otherness'. Furthermore, it allows for various social, material, discursive and experiential elements to be taken into account. Importantly, the concept of 'other' is not inherently concerning. In food studies, for example, notions of 'alternatives' to contemporary food systems have been heralded (see Goodman et al., 2011 and Kneafsey et al., 2008 for examples of literature on alternative food movements). So, far from being a foregone conclusion, questions of 'other' also present opportunities for the exploration of whether that 'other' may or may not be socially acceptable. The importance of the concept of 'other' to the question of acceptability lies in two particular aspects: first, it relates to a question of the acceptability of this 'other' system in and of itself (compared to more common food acquisition methods); second, it relates to how far this 'other' constitutes exclusion from more common methods of food acquisition (as opposed to presenting a socially acceptable alternative).

The concept of 'other' is drawn on to analytically frame Chapter Four, and provides opportunities for several distinct layers of enquiry into the data collected. At a systemic level, it is possible to assess how the systems work in relation to the most common and socially accepted mechanism of food acquisition – commercial food markets through shopping (Meah, 2013) – and to interpret the values embedded within those systems or the foodstuffs themselves. Drawing on literature that both explores and problematises notions of othering in the context of poverty, food and charity research (Cloke et al., 2010; Lister, 2004; Midgley, 2014), the book explores the discursive and experiential aspects of the 'othering' dynamics within emergency food provision. This enables an exploration of the complexities at work in these systems and how organisational motivations and impacts on recipients interact. Midgley (2014) and Cloke et al. (2010) provide opportunities for exploring and problematising the notion of 'other', and draw attention to the moral and market-based qualities embedded within emergency food systems. At the same time, Lister's (2004) work facilitates an appreciation of the importance of discourse in the process and lived experience of othering, particularly through constructs of the 'needy' or 'hungry'.

Sustainability

The normative content is also explored in Chapter Five in relation to the question of the sustainability of food availability and accessibility through emergency food systems; that is, whether emergency food systems are adequately sustainable modes of food acquisition. Comment 12 (CESCR, 1999) states that '"sustainability" incorporates the notion of long-term availability and accessibility'. While the right to food refers to the longevity of sustainability stretching into future generations, this book emphasises sustainability into the medium and longer term of individual or household food insecurity experiences. The sustainability of food access is embedded throughout the right to food, and is also located within obligations to fulfil the right to food – to provide access when a person's means are not adequate enough to ensure it. The question of sustainability is explored in relation to both the availability and accessibility of food in emergency food systems – by assessing the ability of these systems to make food available on the one hand, and the accessibility of that food to those in need of it on the other.

These issues are explored by utilising the concept of power as agency, where power is defined as the ability to exercise agency (Elder-Vass, 2010; Scott, 2001). This concept of agency is employed to understand projects' ability to exercise agency in order to obtain sufficient amounts of food, and the agency of people in need to access that food. Agency is a particularly helpful concept for exploring these issues, as it presents opportunities for examining the impact of structures and the ways in which these may or may not constrain actors' agency. The concept is drawn on to shape the analysis in Chapter Five in relation to the ways in which emergency food providers are able to make food available, particularly within their operational context of the food retail system structure. It is also used to explore individuals' agency in terms of accessing that food –in relation to both accessing projects and accessing enough food inside those projects. By engaging the concept of agency with the work of Poppendieck (1998) and Tarasuk and Eakin (2005) in emergency food studies, the book sheds light on the sustainability of provision in particularly important ways. As found in the work of Tarasuk and Eakin (2005) in Canada, the lack of recipient rights is a key barrier to the agency of recipients in UK emergency food provision; furthermore, as in the US, several of Poppendieck's (1998) 'deadly "ins"' of food charity are identifiable in the UK – notably the instability of food supply and its inaccessibility to potential recipients.

Exploring emergency food provision in relation to obligations set out by the right to food

The obligations that the right to food places on the state to 'respect, protect and fulfil' the human right to food are explored in Chapters Six and Seven through the theme of responsibility. Responsibility is a useful lens through which to assess the notion of states' obligations and the question of the role of all actors (individuals, communities, charities and the private sector) in the progressive realisation of the human right to food. Situating the obligations placed on states – necessarily, given that they are the ones held accountable to these rights – alongside an appreciation of the roles of a full range of societal actors means the theme of 'responsibility' can usefully be employed to explore the questions of who is assuming which responsibilities now, who should be assuming responsibilities, and how might they do that. The theme of responsibility is explored through two particular questions around the role of charity and the role of the state in respecting, protecting and fulfilling the right to food.

The role of charity

The question of the role of charity is first explored in Chapter Six, using the concept of 'care'. The concept of care is specifically employed in relation to 'care ethics' in reference to 'a critical ethic of care and responsibility' (Lawson, 2007, p.2), which sees care 'as a form ethics' (Popke, 2006, p.506). Framed as such, this concept enables the book to explore the phenomenon of emergency food in more depth. Lawson (2007, p.3) argues that care ethics can extend research based on justice as a universal right in light of the way in which they address 'the specific sites and social relationships that produce the need for care and that frame the specific content of care ethics'. Through foregrounding 'the centrality and public character of care activities', Lawson (2007, p.5) argues that responsibility is reframed by care ethics as collective, challenging the ways in which neoliberal approaches have marginalised care and privatised responsibility. This is particularly important for this book, enabling as it does the opportunity for more detailed exploration of how charitable emergency food provision may be assuming responsibility for care for those in food insecurity as a consequence of neoliberal shifts in state-funded provision (indeed, as an example of this marginalisation and privatisation). Lawson's call for embodied caring practices (the giving of emergency food, in this case) to be analysed as multi-sited is also particularly helpful, as it highlights the role of structures, institutions, organisations, communities and individuals in providing care through emergency food provision and shaping definitions and understandings of need and success.

The concept of care is employed to explore the question of the role of charity in relation to how emergency food providers are assuming responsibility for caring for people in food insecurity – and, while they are doing so, how they conceptualise the need for and success of their provision. The questions of who should be taking on these caring responsibilities, and the role charity might have within the context of progressive realisation of the right to food, are then explored. Engaging with care ethics literature enables the research to highlight the ways in which need for and success of UK emergency food provision can be understood as multi-sited. Need and success are often framed by urgency (acute crisis need) and immediacy (meeting immediate need). However, they can be better understood as crisis needs that are situated on a broader spectrum of vulnerability and financial insecurity, and as charitable organisations which also provide support at individual and community levels, as part of much wider welfare networks. This literature also serves to highlight the complexity embedded in notions of responsibility for helping people in food insecurity and realising the right to food, and how states will need to work alongside other actors and stakeholders.

The role of the state

The question of the role of the state is explored through the concept of social protection. Social protection is key to the realisation of the human right to food, particularly in relation to 'fulfilment' of the right. In recent writings on social protection and the right to food, previous UN Rappoteur Olivier DeSchutter refers to 'social protection, social insurance or social security' (DeSchutter and Sepùlveda, 2012). Social protection in these forms has a vital role to play in realising the right to food, and provides an important policy tool for states – particularly with respect to the rights of the 'poorest and most disadvantaged' (DeSchutter, 2012a). DeSchutter and Sepùlveda (2012) further detail the relationship between social protection and the right to food and its twofold importance; that is, it involves fulfilling the right to food in a non-stigmatising way that promotes dignity, and it relieves both immediate hunger and the threat of hunger in the future (DeSchutter and Sepùlveda, 2012, p.6). Relating to this work by the rapporteurs and to the theoretical framework of care, this book also posits that state-provided social protection is an important form of public caring from a right to food perspective.

The relationship between emergency food provision and state-provided social protection (that is, private and public caring) is seen to be particularly important, based on previous research and international experiences indicating that welfare and other state social policies can play a particularly important role in the development and entrenchment of emergency food systems (Poppendieck, 1998; Riches, 2002). Writing elsewhere by DeSchutter (2013, p.4), however, indicates that social protection might also be conceptualised more broadly; he refers to ensuring access to food through 'social protection, whether informally through community support or through State-administered redistributive mechanisms'. However, while DeSchutter (2013, p.4) highlights the importance of informal, community-based social protection, from a right to food perspective the state is seen as the ultimate duty-bearer for ensuring the right is protected, respected and fulfilled for all. Within a right to food context, universality, rights and entitlements are also important – particularly in relation to the fulfilment of the right to food when people are unable to access food for themselves. Food charity, then – insofar as it is neither universal nor an entitlement – poses a challenge to the right to food approach.

This broader concept of social protection does, however, provide the opportunity for considering the role of different types of non-state providers in social protection –particularly important given the Christian nature of The Trussell Trust and many FareShare Community Food Members. Previous research has suggested that some churches involved in food-bank provision feel that food banking in the context of a reduced welfare state may present churches with a renewed role in social protection (Lambie-Mumford, 2013).

The concept of social protection (as public care) and its relationship to the role of the state is explored in particular in Chapter Seven, in relation to the impact that the currently changing welfare state is having on the need for and shape of food banking in the UK today. Chapter Seven also draws on this concept to explore the question of social protection more broadly and the role for a range of actors therein. Bringing social policy literature relating to the (changing) UK welfare state to bear on this part of the book is a particularly important contribution of this chapter. In addition to setting the rise of emergency food provision in this important social and policy context, it serves to problematise prevailing understandings of this welfare retrenchment and its social consequences as inevitable (drawing on, for example, Hay, 2005; Farnsworth, 2011). Furthermore, this literature helps to raise bigger questions about the relationship between the welfare state and emergency food provision in the UK into the future, and facilitates the exploration of several possible future alternatives.

Conclusion: food insecurity and the right to food

Food insecurity is seen as a way of understanding the 'problem' and lived experiences that underpin the need for emergency food provision. The right to food, however, is more than the resolution of that problem. While overcoming food insecurity is a prerequisite for the realisation of the right to food, it is more than this: it is a social ethic, it represents a commitment to the right to food for all as a social good, and it establishes responsibility and a framework (as parent of law and action and in the form of 'progressive realisation') for the continual improvements of societies towards the realisation of the right for all.

FOUR

Food charity: the 'other' food system

This chapter explores the question of whether receiving food from emergency food providers is an *acceptable* process of obtaining food, by right to food standards. It does so by exploring the nature of this provision in the cases under study and exploring key elements of how food is sourced by and acquired from them. In particular, the chapter explores whether emergency food provision as it is emerging in the UK forms a recognisably 'other' system of obtaining food, and considers critically what this might mean for the realisation of the human right to food in the UK.

The analysis presented here is framed by two particular sets of arguments. In the first instance, evidence from this research is combined with previous findings from Tarasuk and Eakin (2005) to discuss how far emergency food provision forms an identifiably 'other' system of food acquisition. Comparing key characteristics of these charities (including the lack of recipient rights, recipient neediness and food operating outside the market) with the most readily accepted form of obtaining food – through shopping – indicates that they do form distinctly 'other systems'.

However, theoretical and empirical evidence from Cloke et al. (2010) and Midgley (2014) also provides an analytical framework for exploring other data collected, which highlights the dynamic social and market-based qualities embedded in these systems. Cloke et al.'s (2010, p.101) work on organisational ethics – 'the performance of organisational ethos' – provides a framework for identifying the moral imperatives on which these systems are based, including 'feeding the hungry' and 'preventing food waste'. Beyond these identifiable social qualities, Midgley's (2014) work also helps to identify how the foods provided in these systems could still be said to contain recognisable market qualities, through discourses of surplus and the donation of privately purchased foods. However, as further data shows us, while identifiable moral and market-based qualities do reside within these systems, this does not necessarily compensate for the ways in which they are experienced as 'other' by those who have to turn to them – and who are then themselves 'othered' through their participation in them.

The chapter argues that ultimately these organisations do make up an identifiably and experientially 'other' system of obtaining food. This 'otherness' is highly problematic when exploring notions of 'acceptability' in a right to food context, which prioritises relatively defined social acceptability and social justice in food experiences. The findings suggest that emergency food provision is not an acceptable means of food acquisition by these right to food standards, in light of its recipients' lived experiences of social unacceptability (embodied in feelings of shame and embarrassment) and exclusion (from socially accepted modes of acquiring food).

Identifying an 'other' system

In order to begin an exploration of whether emergency food provision represents an acceptable way of obtaining food, we must first explore how people in the UK today obtain food. As Meah (2013, p.197) observes, in western societies, shopping is the most common way that people obtain food: 'foodstuffs are distributed through a commercial system and acquired through shopping'. This fact forms the critical premise of the chapter. Participating in the commercial process of shopping defines food experiences in the UK today, and this market-based experience (where people exercise choice and consumer power) is the socially recognised way in which people acquire food for themselves and their families. Understanding this is critical for assessing the social acceptability of emergency food systems. Part of the question of social acceptability, and inherent within the definitions of both food insecurity and the right to food adopted in this book, is the issue of social justice. Being unable to access socially recognised ways of obtaining food because of a lack of money is an important experience of exclusion and social injustice.

How does the emergency food provision undertaken by the organisations under study compare to this mainstream model of food acquisition? Tarasuk and Eakin (2005, p.184) refer to surplus food redistribution through food banks in Canada as representing a 'secondary food system [which] functions outside the "rules" of the competitive food retail system'. While their analysis focused on how key features of food-banking systems enable the distribution of surplus food, the notion that such charitable systems are outside of retail systems – and thereby outside the rules that constitute them – is an important means of understanding both of the case study organisations for this research.

The operation of both organisations outside of both the market and the commercial system in which food is acquired through shopping is a key defining feature of how emergency food provision works. The food is sourced for and acquired from these projects through mechanisms other than market exchange. Food is sourced either through donations of surplus or private donations of previously purchased goods and acquired free, following a process of a recipient being identified as needy – by either attending a project or being referred there.

Food recipients, not consumers

The ways in which the distinction between the experience of people in emergency food systems and the experience of consumers in food retail markets manifests is worth discussing here. According to Tarasuk and Eakin (2005, p.184) the experience of food-bank clients:

> stands in stark contrast to the mainstream food system, where affluent consumers can choose from among literally thousands of different (or seemingly different) food products, marketers bombard them with claims about the virtues of particular product ingredients, and values such as visual perfection, freshness and convenience reign supreme.

Instead of active consumers, people accessing emergency food providers are recipients of food, who qualify for that provision in light of their neediness. Similarly, compared to consumers (for whom retailers make shopping as convenient as possible), recipients of emergency food occasionally have to go to significant lengths to obtain this food – including referral procedures and physically accessing projects in specific places and at specific times. The lack of recipients' rights (both to access projects and when within these systems) and the reliance on volunteer labour forces further distances the emergency food system from that of commercial markets and social security provision.

Outside market exchange

By operating outside of the market, this provision could be said to form an 'other' food system, distinct from the mainstream ways in which people source food in the UK today. Tarasuk and Eakin (2005, pp.177–8) referred to the redistribution of surplus through food banks as forming a 'second tier', 'ad hoc secondary food system'. While most food banks do not redistribute surplus and therefore would not necessarily qualify in this conceptualisation, the situation of both organisations' modes of obtaining food (from Community Food Members of FareShare and Trussell Trust Foodbank Network) outside of market exchange, food commerce and shopping means that these emergency food organisations nevertheless constitute an 'other' system of food acquisition, outside of the socially accepted mainstream.

However, while it is possible to identify and characterise this system as inherently 'other' to the mainstream ways in which people obtain food in the UK, other writing and empirical research suggests that more nuance may lie behind this categorisation. The work of Cloke et al. (2010) and Midgley (2014) indicates that these systems are not completely removed from the commercial food system in light of the market-based qualities that still reside with the food itself, and that the moral imperatives that drive the organisations mean these systems embody social motivations of value.

Moral imperatives in emergency food systems

In studying the nature of emergency food organisations and the local projects that provide food, the moral imperatives that drive and shape the nature of their work become immediately apparent. In exploring these dynamics, it is possible to draw insight from the work of Cloke et al. (2010) on organisational ethos and ethics in relation to homeless charities.

In the first instance, Cloke et al.'s (2010, p.101) analytical framework of organisational ethics – defined as 'the performance of organisational ethos' – provides a way of identifying this moral imperative (as part of the ethos of the case study organisations). In the second, it provides a means of seeing the ways in which these organisations work as a performance of this ethos. As we will see, from the perspective of the providers and those involved in the case study organisations these moral motivations and performances give the systems inherent value.

Organisational missions and motivations

For both organisations, the aim to feed 'hungry' people is a central motivation to their missions. The term 'hunger' is employed in the aims of both organisations to convey their motivation to meet need. The overall mission of The Trussell Trust Foodbank Network is described as being to 'create a nation where nobody needs to go hungry' (Foodbank Network Director). While The Trussell Trust mission maintains a singular focus on feeding hungry people (sometimes discussed as supporting people in crisis: Trussell Trust, n.d.c), for FareShare the moral underpinning of their system is twofold: 'fighting hunger, tackling food waste' (FareShare, n.d.b).

Having said this, while the Trussell Trust Foodbank Network focuses on hunger, it is also a faith-based organisation; its motivation is derived from the Christian basis on which it was established. Sharing Jesus' love (not through proselytising, it must be said, but through the gesture of care) is as important an aspect of its work as the giving of emergency food. The premise on which these projects work is described as: 'Food banks shows Jesus' love in action by giving food to people in crisis in the local area, providing short term emergency relief' (cited in Lambie, 2011, p.13). Faith is embedded in the principles of the network: 'to love and cherish and reach out to our hungry neighbour, people who are in need' (Trussell Trust Foodbank Network Manager). Specific biblical passages on helping the 'hungry' and people experiencing poverty or suffering ultimately drive the work of individual projects – particularly Matthew 25:35–40: 'I was hungry and you fed me'.

Importantly, however, these motivations can also be seen as moral imperatives. For both organisations, hunger – and, in the case of FareShare, food waste – is seen as unjust. As one Trussell Trust Regional Development Officer said regarding why food banks are established: 'I think it's genuine people who have a heart for the community, see the poverty and think, "We just can't stand by and watch this happen"'. Where food banks identify Isiah 58 as a specific motivating passage (see Lambie, 2011), the faith-based moral imperative is particularly clear: 'remove the chains of oppression and the yoke of injustice, and let the oppressed go free. Share your food with the hungry and open your homes to the homeless poor' (Isiah 58:6–7).

The notion of the Foodbank Network as the enactment of this moral imperative, driven by God, is also part of the narrative of how emergency food provision came to be:

> I guess what I'm saying is, food banks were very timely and as a Christian organisation we'd say God knew and God knows. That's why we were, in our view provoked to do something about trying to replicate in 2004, that's when we knew we needed to do it. (Trussell Trust interviewee)

The dual-focused mission of FareShare also enacts particular moral imperatives to overcome hunger and to prevent food waste, as described by their CEO: 'Our vision is that no good food goes to waste. Success, for us, really looks like that all food that is surplus within the UK supply chain gets diverted and fed to people in need, before it becomes waste'.

Moral imperatives – to overcome hunger and food waste – are therefore embedded within the motivations of both organisations. These moral imperatives are in turn enacted through the performance of the systems that have been established for redistribution (to prevent hunger and food waste, in the case of FareShare) and food provision (to prevent hunger and share God's love, in the case of the Trussell Trust Foodbank Network).

Enacting moral imperatives through emergency food systems

The Trussell Trust Foodbank Network provides a particularly insightful example of how these moral imperatives are enacted through organisational ways of working. The moral imperatives driving the Trussell Trust Foodbank Network (overcoming hunger and sharing God's love) are performed through particular practices embedded within the whole food-bank process, and the focus here will be on two of these: the donation of food and the provision of food parcels. The donation of food is discussed as a performance of the moral imperative to relieve hunger and explored in relation to Cloke et al.'s (2010, p.97) concept of 'extra-ordinary kindness' – acts that are beyond 'routine activities of care (for friends, family or neighbours, for example)'. The process of food provision (the act of giving food parcels) can also be seen as a performance of the moral imperative to share God's love, through Cloke et al.'s (2010, pp.14–17, p.97, p.99) notion of 'evangelism through acts' and non-interventionist faith-based approaches where people are provided spaces to just 'be'.

In the first instance, the moral imperative to relieve hunger is enacted through the whole process of food-bank projects, but the performance of donating food to food banks is a particularly interesting site to explore as a performance of this moral imperative – both by those who are running the provision and those donating to it. Private food donation – the main way in which the Foodbank Network food banks access food – is treated here as a distinct site within the wider food-banking 'process'. It can be understood as a preliminary step in the process, necessarily undertaken before provision, which involves a range of actors (supermarket shoppers, congregations, schools and staff at local businesses). The performance of donation specifically can be understood as the performance of this moral imperative through understanding the gesture as an aforementioned act of 'extra-ordinary' kindness (Cloke et al., 2010). Seen in this way, food banks provide a system for giving within which people can perform an act driven by the moral imperative against hunger: donating food.

Food-bank managers and strategic Trussell Trust personnel conceptualise the process of donation as relational; an embodiment of generosity and demonstration of care. The below quote from the Foodbank Network Director illustrates the relational qualities embedded within privately donated food stuffs: generosity; coming from all different walks of life; responding to meet need, actively participating and becoming part of the process. These qualities become embodied within the individual food stuffs:

> I think the key is, as more clients come in, more food comes in, which is amazing and we're very thankful for the public in the UK for their amazing generosity – facilitated through national supermarket collections and all kinds of different schools, churches and everything. The public has been so generous and as that need's increased, the food donations have mirrored that, which is amazing. If there is any good news in this story of the increasing use of food banks, it's that more people have clearly wanted to donate and have felt more engaged in the process of helping a local person in crisis. (Trussell Trust Foodbank Network Director)

It could be argued, then, that the donating of food to food banks provides a key mechanism through which people can perform a moral imperative to relieve hunger. The Foodbank Network makes this mechanism available, thus providing means of participation within this morally driven system.

The moral imperative to share God's love is also performed in these systems through the processes of giving food parcels. While the data suggests that the provision of food is a performance of faith, this performance seems to be enacted in a very particular way. Interviewees went to considerable lengths to emphasise that there was no proselytising at food banks; that religion wasn't 'rammed down people's throats'. Instead, the performance enacted through this process appears to be more closely aligned with the 'evangelism through acts' that Cloke et al. (2010, p.99) observed at soup runs.

The data provides clear demonstrations of how Foodbank Network practices can be seen as a representation of evangelism through action and service. This was particularly the case for the ways Foodbank Network interviewees described how religious practice (prayer or engagement with the gospel) was not part of how the projects ran from recipients' perspectives. Rather, enacting faith lies behind project motivations and forms a key part of the work – they are called to love and bless people through the practice of provision. As one Foodbank manager put it: 'we are motivated by our faith, we don't ram it down people's throat or anything like that but if you cut us open, that's what you find'. While the faith basis therefore becomes embodied, the motivation for recipients to come to an understanding of God or faith is explicit in the hopes of some food-bank managers, for the outcomes of their work: 'There are many other things that I hope people get, my faith, I hope people understand that God loves them when they're having a bad time. I mean things in my faith that come into play in my thinking but I don't necessarily articulate' (East Bristol Foodbank Manager).

The data provides evidence of this non-interventionism (characteristic of 'evangelism as action') and the ways in which the practices aim to provide places of comfort, kindness and spaces to just be. The notion that food is given in a supportive and comforting social space was crucial for interviewees:

> I hope it makes a difference in as much as we're bringing a little bit of ease during that three days' worth of food that they get. I hope the way that we treat them and you know we try and value them and help them in their embarrassment. I hope that has a positive effect as well. (North Bristol Foodbank Manager)

> We get a lot of comments that the atmosphere is really nice and people don't want to leave, they want to stay and sit and eat cake and have drinks and talk with the volunteers so it must be an inviting place for that, they don't take the food and go. (Gleadless Valley Foodbank Manager)

The network's moral imperative to share God's love is therefore performed through the particular food-bank practices embedded in the providing of food. These findings suggest that moral and social aspects are at work within these systems. This indicates that, while the systems may be identified as 'other', important social dynamics are at work that – from the perspective of those involved in the provision – may have particular value.

Emergency food retaining 'market' qualities

The first half of this chapter set out the ways in which emergency food provision could be seen as comprising an 'other' system. The work of Midgley (2014), however, questions the notion of the 'otherness' of surplus food specifically, on the basis of a study of the qualities embedded within the food being redistributed. This half of the chapter explores her findings in relation to data collected for the research reported on in this book. It considers Midgley's (2014) findings and explores the questions of how detached and distanced the food redistributed within these systems is – and, in particular, the market qualities that food may retain.

Surplus food and market qualities

While Midgley's (2014) research is focused on the qualities of the food itself, this book is interested in the wider dynamics of the nature and performance of emergency food provision as a social and material process. It therefore looks at emergency food provision as a whole, and how it fits within wider socioeconomic contexts. While the qualities that may be ascribed to the food itself are an important part of the story, the emphasis here goes well beyond this to look at the ways in which the provision of emergency food is performed as a whole and the social, political-economic and cultural dynamics with which that performance intersects.

Ultimately, Midgley (2014) challenges the notion of surplus food redistribution systems as inherently 'other'. She argues instead, on the basis of her own research, that systems reflect a 'continuum of food system flows and relationships' (Midgley, 2014, p.1) and that the food is not 'completely removed from market relations' (Midgley, 2014, pp.16–17), but that key market qualities, such as branding, remain embodied within them. Midgley uses a quality framing to assess the qualities ascribed to surplus food in UK redistribution systems and finds that, in the transition to surplus, 'detachment and distancing is not total' (Midgley, 2014, p.6). Furthermore, in transitioning into these distribution systems, the food acquires new qualities – including sociality, facilitation and care (Midgley, 2014, pp.17–18).

Surplus food not wasted food

The data collected for this research could be said to support elements of Midgley's (2014) analysis. Mirroring some of her findings relating to the process of transitioning from the retail market to redistribution initiatives, the data highlights the importance of the surplus discourse itself in protecting market-based qualities – notably in the way it positions it apart from waste. In the data collected from FareShare, discourses of surplus and an emphasis on the usability of the food (which is in date and edible) were found throughout. In this surplus discourse, unsalable foodstuffs were spoken of as the result of benign 'kinks' in the system – an unfortunate consequence rather than a stock of foodstuffs that have been rejected and/or cast away (or that are substandard or low quality). Importantly, the concept of surplus discursively distanced the food products from the idea of waste, which is spoken of in such a way as to imply that it is somehow the next stage along, when nothing is done with surplus. This discursive situating of redistributed food is particularly nuanced, and could be seen as reflecting the contingent, situational and contested contexts in which 'waste' is defined (see Watson and Meah, 2013). But importantly, surplus was arguably used as a discourse for avoiding the 'otherness' of waste.

FareShare interviewees placed considerable emphasis on the fact that the food they redistributed was within date, fit for consumption and a result of kinks or quirks in the food system. The food redistributed by FareShare was described repeatedly as 'all within date, perfectly fit for purpose' (FareShare Trustee and FareShare South West Trustee). Reasons given for it being classified as surplus included packaging having been damaged in transit; misprinted barcodes or mistakes on labels; seasonal packaging, discontinued lines and overproduction. One FareShare depot manager also described how some supermarkets require minimum date lengths for ambient products (for example, three months), and when products do not have that date life left they fail the control criteria and become surplus. This framing ultimately conveyed the notion that what was being redistributed through their practices was perfectly good food, which would otherwise be 'wasted' (or go to landfill or anaerobic digestion). The discourse of surplus was key to this being conveyed, implying this group of foodstuffs was an unfortunate by-product of a less than ideal system, rather than rejected.

The way surplus was discussed involved considerable nuance, and an emphasis on the ways in which the food maintained key qualities important to all consumers. The surplus discourse seems to be employed in such a way as to emphasise the closeness of the food to supermarket standards, as opposed to discarded waste. Several FareShare interviewees explicitly highlighted the distinction between surplus and waste food. It was a subtle distinction, but one that appears to be important in the way quality/value is ascribed to the foodstuffs.

> We should recognise actually that we're not necessarily talking about waste, we're talking about surplus, so if surplus isn't found a home for it becomes waste. (FareShare Trustee and Trustee of FareShare South West)

> It's about good food, that might otherwise go to landfill … So I talk about it being about surplus and waste and that's inevitable in an industry where excellence is such an important value for the consumer. (FareShare Yorkshire Trustee)

In this conceptualisation, then, 'surplus' is intercepted precisely to prevent 'waste'. This framing gives the foodstuffs the status of surplus as a way of distinguishing them from 'waste'. Surplus becomes the step before waste, which appears to be defined by its placement in landfill (the physical process of discarding). This enables the food to retain qualities found within the more mainstream commercial food market, such as branding, freshness and aesthetics.

On the basis of this analysis and previous work by Midgley (2014), it may be that the foodstuffs entering into redistribution systems may not be so far away from – and may retain qualitative links to – the commercial food market. However, the emergency food system as a whole is in fact 'other' in light of a range of characteristics – for example, it being run by volunteers and acquired by the needy – so ultimately, when it transitions into these systems, it becomes part of them. The food itself may not be far away from the commercial systems in which it started, but it is nonetheless no longer within them.

Emergency food experienced as 'other'

The findings presented so far suggest that, while the system of emergency food provision could be identified as distinctly 'other' to the mainstream ways in which people obtain food in the UK today, the emergency food and the systems that process it have embedded within them moral imperatives and market-based qualities of value. Identifying such a system as 'other' is not the same as providing a judgement on that system; it leaves open the question of whether this otherness or alternativeness is a good or a bad thing. To explore this notion by right to food standards, much emphasis must be placed on the experience of such systems from the perspective of those accessing them for help with food. Are they experienced as socially just and acceptable, and are they progressive in the ways in which they enable people to access food? These questions form the focus of this section.

Stigma and embarrassment

Ultimately, evidence suggests that emergency food systems are experienced as 'other' by those who turn to them, and findings relating to experiences of stigma and embarrassment indicate this is a difficult experience for those involved. Such embarrassment or stigma – often conceptualised around the moment of 'crossing the threshold' or 'going through the door' – clearly highlight this. This conceptualisation is in itself interesting, and could be seen as representing a movement into the 'otherness' of this system.

> The second thing of course, is it takes an enormous step for anybody to say, 'I need help, I don't know what to do now, about food tonight'. There's no way that you would just think, 'Ah, it's a bit of a freebie, I will nip around the corner and get some'. (Trussell Trust interviewee)

> It's not nice, having to rely on other people but it comes in helpful when there's nothing else, I'd rather take help rather than have my children go hungry. (Emergency food recipient)

These quotes highlight the alienation embedded in various stages of the emergency food process from the perspective of potential recipients. The quote from a Trussell Trust member of staff conveys the difficulties involved in realising that help might be needed, and in admitting that to a charitable provider. The quote from the emergency food recipient highlights the disempowering lack of choice about whether or not to access this provision, especially when looking after others' wellbeing. There is already much evidence of the experience of embarrassment and stigma among those who have to access emergency food provision (see Lambie-Mumford, 2013; Poppendieck, 1998; Tarasuk and Eakin, 2005); this forms a particularly problematic aspect of the provision from a right to food perspective. These findings suggest that the 'otherness' of emergency food provision is not only experienced as socially unacceptable, but also represents an exclusion from the mainstream commercial food market, where people are left with no choice but to receive charitable emergency help.

Material otherness

Questions can also be raised about the material 'otherness' or difference of the experience of acquiring food from emergency food providers; specifically, in terms of the experience of obtaining food from religious spaces as opposed to at a supermarket or other commercial space. Some of the projects visited for the research were located in church buildings. As such, even if the relational experience inside is free from religious discourse, recipients are still required to enter a space which is in itself religious. Figures 3–5 provide examples of religious food-bank distribution centres in particular.

Figures 3 and 4 show buildings in which two different food banks distributed food parcels. Obtaining food from these projects involved going into a church building, which was highly visible as such, with prominent signs and religious symbols or messages on them. Some of

Figure 3: Food-bank centre in a religious building with doorbell access

these buildings may also have physical barriers to entry; in the case of the building in Figure 3, recipients are required to press a bell and wait for a volunteer to let them in. As is common practice for Trussell Trust Foodbank distribution centres, when a session is open, a food-bank

Figure 4: 'Food bank open' signs make access conspicuous

sign is placed outside the building so people know where to go (see Figure 4). A consequence of this is that people entering the building to obtain food parcels are conspicuous as food-bank recipients.

Figure 5 depicts an example of a room in which food-bank parcels are distributed. Further to the importance of having to step into formally religious buildings is the materiality of the rooms in which food is distributed. In many instances, these spaces incorporate religious images or symbols; in Figure 5, the room is set out for a food-bank session and is part of a small chapel on the site of a larger church.

The lack of substantive data from recipients makes it impossible for this study to assess how they experience the materiality of the spaces in which emergency food is provided. What this analysis is able to illustrate is just how different the materiality of emergency food project spaces is, compared to mainstream commercial outlets. This analysis raises a question for future research: is the moral imperative of sharing God's love – even when it is, in practice, non-proselytising – ultimately

Figure 5: Food-bank centre in a chapel laden with religious imagery

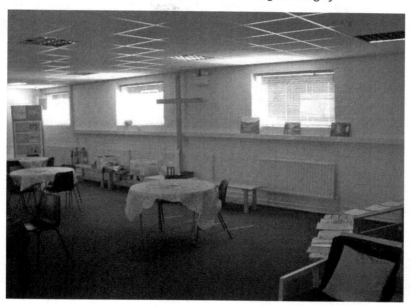

a disempowering experience of 'other' due to the materiality of the religious spaces in which it is enacted?

Othering through language and disempowerment

A key dimension of how emergency food provision is experienced relates to notions of exclusion. Previous research on food poverty highlights the social exclusion embedded within the experience of not being able to access food from mainstream sources, or having to access it in constrained ways due to lack of financial resources (Dowler et al., 2001; Hitchman et al., 2002). The data collected for this research highlighted particular elements of exclusion attributed to accessing these systems in relation to experiences of othering and disempowerment.

Building on the work of Lister (2004) on othering with respect to poverty, the ways in which 'neediness' or 'hungry' are constructed in these systems could be a way in which those accessing emergency food are 'othered through language' (Lister 2004, p.100). In particular, moral imperatives to 'feed the hungry' could construct recipients as 'passive objects of concern' (Lister, 2004, p.115). Furthermore, the ways in which 'need' for emergency food is constructed is arguably an additional othering process when people are identified as 'needy' and 'in need' of emergency food provision by definition of their exclusion from, or lack of access to, mainstream commercial food systems.

A further element of exclusion experienced within these systems is that of disempowerment. Recipients' lack of agency, in terms of both accessing mainstream commercial food systems and within emergency systems themselves, can be particularly disempowering. This leads to the subject of the next chapter, regarding power and agency both of and within emergency food systems; but it is important here in relation to the disempowering nature of the experience of emergency food provision, and the experience of needing that provision as a result of exclusion from mainstream systems.

The nature of emergency food provision as 'other' was established early on in this chapter. In critically assessing the consequences of these systems' 'otherness', the findings presented indicate that the experience can be problematic by right to food acceptability standards, given the lived experiences of social unacceptability and exclusion. In the first instance, the material otherness of this provision – in terms of accessing this food from places very distinct from commercial outlets – is particularly important for understanding the nature of the 'otherness' of these systems. Furthermore, the ways in which the need for and experience of these systems are embarrassing and disempowering for recipients is also important, with significant consequences for how these systems can be seen in right to food terms.

Conclusion

The central preoccupation of this chapter has been to ascertain whether emergency food systems represent a distinctly 'other' system to the mainstream, socially acceptable means by which people access food in the UK today, and to critically assess the nature of this system. In the first instance, this chapter concludes that emergency food provision does constitute a distinctly 'other' system of food acquisition, which sits very much apart from the mainstream ways in which most people access food today (namely, commercial markets and shopping).

The processes of obtaining this food have been shown to be distinctly 'other': given to needy people, as opposed to chosen by active consumers, and outside mechanisms of economic exchange. The data presented here, as well as work by other scholars, illustrates many layers of nuance to this 'othering' process. Embedded within these systems are qualities that still link to the market (such as branding), as well as moral imperatives driving the work of these organisations. Indeed,

Midgley (2014, p.7) suggests these practices are analytically constructed as 'other', rather than empirically so.

On the basis of this research, however, it is concluded here that there is in fact something distinctly and unavoidably 'other' about this provision – both in terms of its performance (of food sourcing and provisioning and the ways in which that provision is accessed) and in the discourse of need and hunger embedded within it, given Lister's (2004, p.122) highlighting of the 'power of discourse … in constructing 'the poor' as 'different' or 'Other''. These systems are also different from, for example, receiving left-overs from friends or family – in light of the power dynamics embedded within emergency food provision and the recipients' 'needy' circumstance. Furthermore, and more importantly still, while the emergency food system might be identifiable as 'other', it is also experienced as other and as a significant form of social exclusion.

The second conclusion of this chapter rests on the question of whether this 'other' system could be said to be acceptable, by right to food standards. Ultimately, the otherness of emergency food provision is the critical factor in assessing the acceptability of the experience of obtaining food through emergency food provision. The beginning of the chapter set up what a mainstream food acquisition experience looks like in the UK today. These experiences are dominated by commercial markets and most food being obtained through shopping (Meah, 2013). The neediness of emergency food recipients embodies their exclusion from this mainstream food experience – and therein lies the problem for acceptability: the social injustice of exclusion from such social food 'norms' is key. In emergency food systems, individuals become receivers of food rather than purchasers and selectors of food – stripped of their agency and choice (a key value in the contemporary food system in the UK). While the increasing prominence of emergency food provision in media and public discourses may aim to spread information about how these work, in the hope of overcoming some of the stigma or marginalisation attached to these initiatives, they nonetheless remain very different experiences of obtaining food from those enjoyed by people who are not in poverty or financial crisis. This is the central concern of a right to food analysis: the lack of choice, vulnerability, neediness and otherness of the experience of emergency food are highly problematic.

FIVE

The sustainability of food charity

Sustainability, by right to food standards, requires adequate amounts of food to be accessible in the short, medium and longer term. As a practical response to the problem of food insecurity, this means that, in emergency food systems, both the ability of emergency providers to make enough food *available* in the immediate and longer terms, and the ability of recipients to *access* this food through these organisations now and into the future, are important points of analysis. To explore whether this is true of the systems emerging in the UK, this chapter explores questions of availability and accessibility through an analytical framework of power.

For the purposes of this chapter, power is seen as the 'capacity for exercising agency' (Elder-Vass, 2010, p.87). For questions of sustainability (as the availability and accessibility of emergency food), the agency of emergency food providers to secure a food supply and the agency of people in need to access it are particularly important points for empirical exploration. Given the importance of structure embedded within the conceptualisations and definitions of food insecurity and the right to food adopted for the book, agency (as power) is also understood here to occur within the context of structures that shape it. In particular, this chapter explores the agency of emergency food providers to make food available within the structures of the food system on the one hand, and the agency of people to access that food within the structures of emergency food provision on the other. In arriving at conclusions from the findings presented, the work of Poppendieck (1998) on the 'seven deadly "ins"' of emergency food – notably, instability and inaccessibility – is drawn on.

In exploring the agency of emergency food providers to make food available, this chapter focuses on the relationship between these organisations and the wider food system by exploring their agency in relation to two key aspects of this dynamic: in sourcing food; and in corporate partnerships and future planning. The direct sourcing of food is clearly imperative for emergency food organisations to make food available now and into the future, but – as will become apparent in this chapter – corporate partnerships with food retailers and others are also important aspects of how these organisations are able to operate now, and are shaping the way they will operate into the future.

To come to a better understanding of people's agency to access the food available in these projects, this chapter looks at the relationship between those potential recipients and the emergency food systems they are (trying to) access – in terms of both the processes of accessing this provision and the available mechanisms for exercising agency when they are within these systems. The ways in which particular processes and related factors facilitate or block the exercising of agency to access this provision are examined; for example, referral processes, opening times and limits on how many times someone can receive support. Principles that are lacking in these systems (notably, rights for recipients and accountability of charitable organisations) are also seen as important factors relating to people's agency when they are in these systems, as these would provide formal levers for recipient power.

Organisational agency in the food system

Food sourcing for sustained availability

The ability to source food for distribution (through securing either surplus or private donations) and to ensure ongoing practice to distribute that food underpin the capacity and sustainability of the work of both case study organisations. This chapter analytically situates an assessment of these elements within the context of the wider structures of the food system, given the important ways in which these organisations are situated therein.

In terms of food sourcing, for FareShare, surplus food is taken from within the food chain and so is inherently tied up with the wider system; for the Trussell Trust Foodbank Network, food is largely donated by individual donors, but national food drives (whereby food is collected from customers at national supermarket chain stores across the country on a set weekend) have become increasingly important ways of soliciting those donations. This food sourcing can be situated more particularly within the food retail structure in the UK, given the predominant role played by food retailers in providing access to both food surplus and retail customers on a nationwide scale. Organisations' ability to ensure ongoing practice can also be situated within the context of the wider food system, given the importance of corporate partnerships for funding and other forms of in-kind support that facilitate these organisations' work, as will be demonstrated.

The findings presented here suggest that the case study organisations' agency to source food and secure their provision in the longer term is shaped by the structures of the food industry – particularly the food retail system in the UK. They indicate that, while both organisations take strategic approaches to food sourcing, FareShare is ultimately dependent on what food is made available to them through retailers' supply chains. Trussell Trust Foodbank Network donations depend on individual giving; however, national food drives and prominent supermarket chains are an increasingly prominent mechanism for the Network to secure donations, bringing important added value to the franchise by saving volunteers' time and energy setting up food drives. In terms of partnerships and planning, the findings indicate that both organisations take a strategic approach to these partnerships and horizon scanning – particularly The Trussell Trust, which appears to take a consciously diversified approach to these agreements. However, the data suggests that the finer points of detail in these partnerships are not necessarily within providers' control, and that these partnerships can have knock-on effects on the shape of ongoing practice and organisational capacity to plan into the future.

These findings have important implications for what we can say about the sustainability of food availability in emergency food systems, given the dangers of both organisations becoming dependent on their relationships with the food retail industry for the sourcing of food. In addition, the lack of control these organisations can exercise over corporate partnerships (including those with food retailers) means their future planning can be limited, and ongoing and future practice (in terms of what they provide and how) can be shaped by the terms of these agreements in potentially unanticipated ways.

FareShare

In the case of FareShare, the findings demonstrate that the majority of surplus food redistributed by the Network is sourced through national-level relationships rather than locally at the depots. In building these national relationships, strategic-level staff have a policy of going 'through' the retailers to 'open up' surplus within their supply chains. The data indicates that the ratios of nationally-to-locally-sourced surplus can vary between depots. Data from the South West depot also suggests that recording systems can imply that arrangements are national when they are actually local (for example, a nationally operating organisation that only delivers to the South West depot). The FareShare CEO talked about how the ratio varies (sometimes 100%, sometimes 80%), but said that most: '[have] a genesis at the national partnership. Which makes sense when you think about the strategy of trying to access that food through the retailers.'

Depots' apparent reliance on national arrangements for sourcing surplus raises several questions for FareShare's agency at different scales of operation. In the first instance, it raises a question of depots' capacity to secure local arrangements: in a food system dominated by national-scale logistics, perhaps it is only at a strategic level that sustainable and practical arrangements can be made? From depots' perspectives, too, issues of capacity in terms of time available to cultivate relationships may be an issue. A second question is raised regarding depots' ability to diversify their food sources – beyond national arrangements – to protect their levels of incoming food. Again, this may be due to the nature of the food system and/or capacity at projects, but the reliance on national-level arrangements indicates that depots have very little agency in determining the nature of their relationships with the food industry. The importance of these questions is highlighted in the following quote, from the manager of a depot that appears to be particularly proactive in locally sourcing surplus:

> Then, locally, we try and do as much as we can, as well, for obvious reasons. Firstly, we need to be sustainable. We need to know that if our national office, for whatever reason, stopped offering us food we could still get food out to our clients. Also, it's the right thing to do. If we can get food from a local area, then it's fewer miles spent. (FareShare South West Operations Director)

FareShare's emphasis on going 'through' retailers to open up mechanisms for surplus further highlights the importance of the ways the food system works for shaping how the case study organisations are forced to work and their agency in determining this. This way of working was consciously reactive; FareShare established practices and ways of working on the basis of how the industry was structured and fitted into those structures: 'My strategy was very much that the most efficient way for us to access a food industry was to reflect the way that the food industry is structured, with the retailers holding that dominant position between the customers and the supply chain' (FareShare CEO).

Despite this very strategic approach, in which national team staff build relationships with the most prominent retailers to open up their extensive supply chains in order to access surplus, the data highlights the fragility of these relationships – from the perspectives of both FareShare depots and the Community Food Members (CFMs) who receive and serve the food. This data highlights the unpredictability of the food supplied this way; FareShare is not able to reliably supply particular volumes or particular types of food, posing challenges for CFMs, who cite frustrations with the unpredictability – and sometimes inappropriateness – of the food they receive.

From the depots' perspective, the findings indicate that, while national-level FareShare staff may be able to develop strategic relationships with and through retailers, control over the outcome of these and how they regularly translate into food received by depots appears limited: 'Luckily, we've never been in a position where we haven't been able to fulfil minimum orders to our projects. So, just some weeks they [CFMs] have lots of choice, and a bit extra, and other weeks it's less so' (FareShare South West Operations Director).

Overall, many CFMs feel FareShare food is beneficial; however, the findings suggest the agency of FareShare is limited, demonstrated by the inappropriateness of food for CFM clients, insufficient and unpredictable types and amounts of food, little flexibility in what CFMs receive and the fact that all CFMs had to source additional food from elsewhere. This data furthermore highlights that CFMs' agency within the structure of the FareShare system is limited to responding to what is on offer and choosing from what is available. CFMs are notified in advance of what is available for them to choose from and how much they will get.

Some interviewees talked about the inappropriateness of some of the foodstuffs they were offered for the kind of project they were or the kind of people they served. For example, the head chef at a large homeless project that provided daily hot breakfasts and lunches said he would rather receive meal ingredients than snacks from FareShare:

> It's OK, it's like I said to you rather than send me six cases of crisps or a box of Polos and a box of KitKats I'd rather it be something more substantial like 20 lb of chuck steak that I can actually use on a lunchtime service rather than, you know, just thinking what am I going to do with six cases of Jelly Babies. (Archer Project, Head Chef)

The manager of Bristol Refugee Rights also raised the issue of culturally appropriate foods and the difficulties their project has handling and distributing non-Halal meat: 'That's one of the things about FareShare for us, that most of the meat we can't use because we only serve Halal food, so that's in terms of meat'.

Interviewees also highlighted the unpredictability and limited volume of food CFMs received weekly. The manager of a sheltered housing scheme discussed the dilemma her team has when there is not enough of a product to share equally among the residents, and indicated that staff might sometimes intercept the food to avoid conflict: 'When you get some things and there's only 12 of them and you've got 14 people and then you've got to make a decision about whether we [the staff] just eat them!' (Emmaus Project Manager).

These quotes highlight CFMs' relative lack of agency in the FareShare structure (choosing from what depots received and can ration out between all their projects), and FareShare's ultimately responsive (to the structure of the UK food system) work. All CFMs visited sourced other food from different sources, either purchasing it with funds or soliciting or benefiting from private donations or other surplus (often on a local shop-by-shop basis). Indeed, this diversified food sourcing approach is necessary, and encouraged in order to avoid dependency:

> The one thing we don't do is create a dependency on FareShare for any charity because we never know what food we can give them, we never know what quantities we've got to give them so to create a dependency would actually put people in more of that food poverty bracket than they are now, so we are really a top-up charity not a whole solution. (FareShare National Head of Operations)

This quote neatly sums up the findings from this section as a whole: FareShare obtains what it can and distributes it between members – but what that food is and how much there is of it (so long as it fulfils food safety standards and other criteria) appears largely beyond their control.

The Trussell Trust

Given the Trussell Trust Foodbank Network's predominant reliance on privately donated foodstuffs and public goodwill, there are some distinctive aspects to the power dynamics within their food sourcing mechanisms. The Network's processes highlight ways in which the food retail structure affects their agency – notably through the Network's arrangements with several of the largest retailers for national food collection days.

Food-banks' agency in food sourcing relies in the first instance on public goodwill to donate food stuffs. In some of the strategic interviews with Trussell Trust personnel, concern was conveyed for a time in the future when food banks and donating food are no longer 'flavour of the month' (Head of Fundraising): 'Who knows how long it will last? What we are going to say is "reap hay when the sun shines". It will not last forever, Hannah, I don't believe, just because of the nature of business' (Trussell Trust Northern Ireland Regional Development Officer (RDO)). Beyond this concern for natural distraction away from the food-bank cause, the Trust's PR and Marketing Manager highlighted a further, foreseeable challenge and its potential impact: 'As you get bigger more people question, challenge and sometimes try to discredit you; you start having conversations with people who are not 100% supportive'.

The Network's ability to maintain levels of food donation is therefore a key challenge into the future. However, its food sourcing mechanisms are shaped in practice by the structure of the food retail system. Through national-level partnerships, Trussell Trust food banks are able to hold collection days at stores throughout the country (with local food banks collecting at their local shops). These arrangements are seen as significantly added value for franchisees, as many projects previously struggled to obtain the authorisation to run them at the individual shop level. However, these are medium- or short-term arrangements, and will be reviewed thereafter:

> But having that – two supermarket things already organised a year, I would pay anything for that. Because the amount of time it took our guy to get into one of the supermarkets, the faff was just so almighty it was ridiculous so it was flipping brilliant, loved it and now we know that every year we have a minimum of two shopping weekends, you know, it's nice on your mind. (Gleadless Valley Foodbank Manager)

> These relationships have big, significant benefits to the ongoing development of food banks. It is certainly a plus when you are talking to community groups and trying to get them to engage with you at the very beginning. (Trussell Trust North Wales RDO)

Given the growth in the number of food banks and amount of food parcels being distributed, national supermarket collections are likely to remain key to the ways in which the Network as a whole, as well as individual food-bank projects, are able to supply themselves with food – and a key determinant of how much volunteer capacity will be required to do so (more, if these drives have to be arranged and publicised locally). The increasing level of knowledge of how a food bank might be run without paying for a franchise also mean these national food drives could become an increasingly important selling point for the Foodbank franchise. Therefore, although in a different way to FareShare, the agency of the Network in sourcing food could also be said to be influenced in important ways by the structure of the food system and the goodwill of food retailers. It appears that this is not only true now, but could be increasingly the case into the future, when both organisations could become more dependent on their relationships with food retailers to source food in the face of ongoing and future need.

Corporate partnerships and future planning

While the findings presented so far discussed organisations' agency in sourcing food for sustained availability, data was also collected relating to their agency in corporate partnerships and future planning. These are also significant factors in ensuring the sustainability of food access, given the ways in which these partnerships (through funding and in-kind support) become part of or enable these organisations' operations. While both organisations had partnerships with a range of private companies, relationships with food industry partners were particularly prominent.

The findings suggest that the case study organisations exercised agency in these partnerships, particularly through: maximising opportunities that present themselves as a consequence of the currently high profile of food assistance and hunger; being clear and forthright in their position when agreeing terms and conditions of partnerships; horizon scanning and planning for when short- and medium-term partnerships end; and diversifying partnership relationships as much as possible to avoid dependency. However, the data raises a question over the agency of the organisations to manage and have authority over the detail of some of these relationships, and the consequences this might have for them as organisations. Two examples discussed here are FareShare running food drives as part of retail partnerships (when their aim is to reduce surplus) and the Foodbank Network taking surplus (when the act of donation is central to its ethos).

FareShare's partnerships with private sector organisations were largely food-industry-based, whereas for the Foodbank Network these varied considerably (including food, banking, logistics and manufacturing sectors). The nature of these partnerships also varied. FareShare's relationship with the food industry centred largely on partners opening up surplus food for them to redistribute; other partners may have sent staff to volunteer or help in other ways. The Foodbank Network's partnerships varied in nature and benefited from staff being mentored by private sector partners' staff, as well as food donations organised at offices and funding. The data indicates that both organisations took strategic approaches to partnership working. Both in the sense of considering the impact on their organisations (and mission), and – particularly in the case of FareShare, but also in The Trussell Trust – operating at a strategic level to solicit these partnerships.

Securing partnerships

Strategic interviewees from both organisations talked about corporate partnerships, their importance and their role. The basis of these partnerships appeared to be varied, involving opening up surplus or food products (for FareShare, and occasionally the Foodbank Network), sending retail partner staff to volunteer (for both case studies) and sharing expertise in the form of mentoring or consultancy (for the Foodbank Network). The ways in which interviewees described processes of securing partnerships, and the practice of these partnerships, revealed several dimensions to their apparent organisational agency and its interaction with food industry structures.

In securing partnerships, the data suggests that the organisations take a strategic approach to maximising the opportunities presented to them as a consequence of the high profile of issues of food assistance and food poverty. The following quotes suggest they may also benefit from the competitive nature of the food retail industry:

> We were well aware that actually although they're ultra-competitive, one of the things that the retailers do all of the time is copy each other. If they see something working then the others pile in there. That's why Asda have done a food drive with Trussell, and both of us have done this partnership with Tesco. (FareShare CEO)

> Five supermarkets have come out and said, 'We want you to do food-bank collections'. ... We did a first national food-bank collection with Tesco. All the Tesco staff got excited because our teams were there talking about the work. Their

teams could talk to our teams and they could then talk to the customers. Some of the other supermarkets visited those projects on that day and saw that and heard it. Now, they all want to do it. (Trussell Trust Operations Director)

These findings seem significant in terms of the case studies' agency in partnership development (at the time of the research). For the Trussell Trust, far from going to lengths to pursue partnerships, 'Because of our profile, a lot of companies have been coming to us now' (Trussell Trust Corporate Partnerships Manager).

In addition to the profile of the case studies and the issue of food poverty, the data suggests they consciously tap into corporate social responsibility agendas when looking to secure partnerships:

We should be saying to food manufacturers and retailers look, we can help you avoid waste, we can help give you lots of corporate social responsibility advantages, brownie points, because we're working with you to minimise waste, we're saving you millions in terms of cost and we're feeding people, how about that? That's pretty good in your annual corporate social responsibility report and that's why Sainsbury's has signed up, that's why Waitrose has signed up, Tesco's has signed up. (FareShare National Trustee and Trustee of FareShare South West)

In the process of securing partnership agreements, it appears that the case study organisations are clear and forthright in their position when agreeing terms and conditions:

We have not gone anywhere where we haven't wanted to go. We have worked on exactly the same ethos as we do with grant funding: 'This is what we do. If you want to fund us to do this, thank you very much. We will have your money. If you come back to us and say, "The conditions are that you change your model here or you do this", which would have a significant impact, then we wouldn't take the funding'. In the same way, we wouldn't take the corporate deal either. (Trussell Trust Head of Fundraising)

No, I think we're challenging them and by working with them we're in a much, much stronger place to influence. The phrase we use internally all the time is, 'We will not help a retailer polish their brand, unless that retailer is committed to and delivering on our agenda'. (FareShare CEO)

The Trussell Trust also appears to be conscious of taking into account the motivations of potential partners, and the knock-on consequences for how productive the relationship is likely to be:

> You've got the ones who want to … When you look at the motivation, some are like, 'We want to engage our staff in something practical and something current, let's do food collections'. Other people are like, 'We really believe in Trussell Trust, we want to invest in you, let's work together and create a partnership that works'. (Trussell Trust Corporate Partnerships Manager)

The data also suggests, however, that the Trussell Trust in particular takes a strategic approach to horizon scanning and planning for when short- and medium-term partnerships come to an end:

> We know that somewhere down the line, the partnership will end. They want to do different things for different people. For us, that is important because it gives us breathing space to get the stuff we need to run, but it also gives us that breathing space to think about what we are going to do when the partnership is [not] there. (Trussell Trust Operations Director)

Furthermore, the Trust also appears to take as diversified an approach as possible to partnership arrangements, to avoid becoming dependent on any particular sets of arrangements:

> I think there are risks. We know there are risks around dependency, being in corporate relationships. But we agreed early on with Tesco's that there was no discussion about exclusivity. So we've got relationships with the other supermarkets, they're warm, they're different. But if one bit goes wrong or whatever, we can ride another horse if we need to. (Trussell Trust Executive Chairman)

The impact of partnerships on ways of working

The findings suggest that the case study organisations take strategic approaches to securing and managing partnership relations, and that they may wield particular power in negotiating these due to the current high public profile of hunger and food banking. However, other data collected raises questions about the power dynamics of these relationships in practice – how tailored they are to the needs of the organisations, and the ways in which knock-on effects may be shaping the organisations in unforeseen or unintended ways. In the case of FareShare, the introduction of food drives to incentivise retail partners is explored; in the case of the Foodbank Network, the ways in which amounts collected at food drives is making them rethink ways of working are discussed.

FareShare began doing food drives (first at Sainsbury's, then at Tesco) as an integral part of their relationship with these retailers. However, this has caused tension among some involved with depots, who feel that food drives undermine their waste message:

> FareShare was fundamentally set up to avoid waste. It was there to deal with surplus. It was not there to do food collections at Sainsbury's and to take food that wasn't waste. (FareShare National Trustee and Trustee of FareShare South West)

> A good example of where they [FareShare's aims] come into conflict would be, for example, doing a food drive with Sainsbury's or Tesco, where the general public are being asked to donate a product, because that's not surplus. However, what that does is enable us to align our brand to retailers in a public way, to their consumers, which has a transformational effect on the supply chain's view and attitude of us. So the ends justify the means in terms of making surpluses [more accessible], and building relationships. (FareShare CEO)

Data from the Trussell Trust Foodbank Network highlights one main area in which corporate partnerships may have influenced decisions to enter into different territory: the receipt of surplus food and product donated in bulk (though not necessarily surplus) directly from manufacturers (see donations from Kellogg's detailed in CEBR, 2013).

The impact of partnership power dynamics on the agency of the case study organisations in their future planning is interesting to note here as well. Interviewees touched on the ways in which partnerships with the food industry in particular are likely to have considerable impact. The Trussell Trust, for example, is rethinking ways of working in response to the volume of food being collected at retail partners' food drives:

> On the side of life with the likes of Tesco and whatnot, it may change our strategic thinking. This has always been a charity that franchises and sets up a local food bank. We are now thinking, and we are only thinking but I am going to say it anyway: 'Do we set logistical hubs up throughout the country?' If we decide to collect from supermarkets, the food could be stored where local charities, not just food banks, could draw down food. It has already been donated by the public. (Trussell Trust Operations Director)

This power dynamic is arguably even more profound for FareShare, which is dependent on food industry relationships (largely opened up for them through relationships with retailers) for the surplus food they are able to distribute. Not being able to predict or be assured of how these relationships and surplus supply will be maintained into the future is particularly problematic for the purposes of future planning; the amount of food distributed is 'all to do with success of securing enough from the food industry' (FareShare CEO).

The vulnerability of food sourcing and corporate partnerships

The findings presented here on organisational agency in ensuring the availability of food through food sourcing and corporate partnerships have provided important insight into how this agency is determined by the structure of the wider food system. In particular, this analysis suggests that, while both organisations take strategic approaches to food sourcing (FareShare through national-level partnerships and agreements and the Trussell Trust through public messages and partnerships with supermarkets to arrange food drives), ultimately these sources are vulnerable and influenced by forces outside organisational control. FareShare is dependent on retailers and their supply partners for opening up the surplus for them to intercept; as the experiences of CFMs imply, they are placed in an ultimately reactive position in terms of the food they are able to provide. While The Trussell Trust's food sourcing is highly diversified, supermarket collection days are an increasingly important mechanism through which their sources are sought.

The findings suggest that the case study organisations adopt strategic approaches to the securing and management of their partnerships. They exercise agency through: maximising the opportunities presented to them; appealing to corporate social responsibility agendas; being clear and forthright when establishing the terms of partnerships; practicing horizon scanning and partnership diversification when looking to the medium- and long-term future. However, the power imbalances embedded within these partnerships have knock-on effects in terms of ongoing practice and organisations' capacity to plan into the future.

These findings are significant, as they highlight the ultimate vulnerability and instability of these organisations' agency for sustainably making food available. Food sourcing is vulnerable to being severely limited where retailers do not grant access to surplus or customers on scales previously enjoyed. The nature of partnership agreements – what they provide to organisations, and at what costs – can also have knock-on effects on organisational capacity to plan into the future, as well as their current ways of working.

Recipient agency in emergency food systems

To assess emergency food systems' sustainability from the perspective of those vulnerable to or experiencing food insecurity, potential recipients' agency to access emergency food when they need it is crucial. By the right to food standard, food must be available and accessible in the short, medium and longer terms. This section explores the question of individuals' agency to access the food available within these systems. Several dynamics are explored and recipients' agency in relation to them is examined. First, the processes and logistics of *gaining access* to emergency food projects are discussed in relation to agency. Then, the key mechanisms in ensuring and enabling *agency within these systems* – accountability and rights – are explored. The findings show that the organisations' lack of accountability, the variable accessibility of projects and the lack of rights and entitlements recipients are attributed mean these systems are not able to provide sustainable sources of support for help with food. As long as people cannot access as much food as they need, for as long as they need, when they need it, and as long as they do not have any rights or way of holding organisations to account within these systems, we must look elsewhere for responses that meet right to food standards.

In terms of practical access issues and people's agency in gaining access to emergency food, both procedural and logistical aspects can be considered. While there is significant variability in terms of how emergency food projects of all kinds operate, particular features are worth discussing here. From the data collected on how national organisations and local projects work, several access processes have the potential to inhibit people's agency to obtain necessary help with emergency food: eligibility criteria; gatekeeping processes; and limits on how much food can be obtained.

Eligibility

Some emergency food projects employ eligibility criteria to a greater or lesser degree. This could be informal: a project targeting a specific group, but not exclusive to them (for example, a meal programme in a homeless project that also allows others in need to attend). Or these criteria could be incorporated more formally. For example, as discussed in Lambie (2011), The Trussell Trust's food-bank processes stipulate that recipients must be within some kind of 'managed process', meaning they are plugged into a system or service that is dealing with and will resolve the crisis that drove them to a food bank. This could mean that particular populations – notably asylum seekers, failed asylum seekers and roofless homeless people – may be excluded from eligibility, on the basis of their situation not necessarily having a resolution and food banks only providing food for limited periods of time.

Gatekeeping and vouchers

In some instances, projects may have gatekeeping processes in place, operating referral systems that people have to go through to access emergency food. This is particularly the case in Trussell Trust food banks, in which the voucher referral system is key to the projects' operation. In order to obtain food from a food bank, a recipient must have a voucher from a partner organisation within the local community; for example, health visiting services, advice centres or schools. This voucher system is also how the 'managed process' criteria is rationalised and operationalised by food banks; those people holding vouchers to distribute are workers at services that would be dealing with or assisting people with the crisis that led them to require emergency food.

These gatekeeping processes are important in terms of people's ability to access emergency food systems for several reasons. First, people need to be accessing mainstream services (such as health, social care and social security services) in order to access food banks. Second, food banks do not necessarily give vouchers to every such service in their local community – relationships are built at their discretion – so people not only have to be accessing mainstream services, but also have to access the *right* (voucher-holding) services.

Limits

Another procedure that could limit people's agency to access emergency food systems is the existence of limits to the amount of help they can receive. The food-bank model has a so-called 'three-voucher rule', which limits the amount of food parcels people can receive to three per crisis (see Lambie-Mumford, 2013). This means that, even when people have accessed the system, they do not necessarily hold the agency to determine how long they receive help for.

Logistical barriers

In addition to the way in which processes impact on people's agency to access help from emergency food systems, logistical aspects can also be considered. The first relates to geography and physical accessibility; there may be a lack of any emergency food projects in certain areas, or a lack of distribution centres in the case of food banks (locations from which food parcels are collected) in places people can reach. Previous research (Lambie-Mumford et al., 2014) highlights the lack of comprehensive, systematic documentation of existing emergency food projects. A further barrier to access may therefore be a lack of knowledge about what projects exist or how to access them.

Further logistical issues may be encountered even for physically accessible projects that people know how to access. Projects and food-bank distribution centres sometimes open only a few times per week, for short periods of time. This may pose logistical issues for people with work or caring commitments. Furthermore, these distribution centres and projects can be in religious settings (as discussed in Chapter Four), which can present a barrier for those who are not religious.

Particular barriers – both logistical and procedural – can therefore potentially limit people's agency in accessing help from emergency systems when they need it. Depending on the structure of these systems, they may reside outside eligibility criteria or not be accessing the services that refer people to projects. Where such referral processes exist, people are unlikely to be able to determine their need for themselves; even when judged to be in need and sent to a project, they may not be able to access it for as long as they feel they require. Physical access barriers may also exist in terms of projects existing locally and being open and accessible at convenient times.

Rights and entitlements

Once people are in these emergency food systems, key aspects that could promote their agency include recipients having rights within the system, and being able to hold the organisations to account. Importantly, within emergency food systems, recipients are not afforded rights; the provision is not seen as an entitlement (see the discussion of Tarasuk and Eakin (2005) in Chapter Four). This contrasts with consumer rights in retail systems and citizens' rights in social security systems. Similarly, these charitable organisations – unlike statutory bodies or, to some limited extent, retailers (in terms of consumer power) – cannot be held accountable to those that require the provision. These emergency food systems lack accountability mechanisms; as such, people within them lack key mechanisms for exercising agency.

These findings mean that people have very little agency in terms of accessing emergency food. Access can be obstructed by processes of referral and eligibility thresholds, as well as logistical issues that form physical barriers to the provision. Once access has been gained, the systems afford recipients very little agency; they are not given rights and have very little recourse to hold organisations to account. As such, access to food through emergency systems is not sustainable from (potential) recipients' perspectives, given their lack of agency when accessing the systems and when seeking the standards of support they require therein.

Conclusion

The findings presented here are significant because they indicate that similar dynamics may be at work in UK-based emergency food systems as Poppendieck (1998) identified in the US. In discussing the findings of her study, Poppendieck (1998, pp.201–30) identified what she called the 'seven deadly "ins" of emergency food': insufficiency; inappropriateness; nutritional inadequacy; instability; inaccessibility, inefficiency; and indignity. Two of these 'ins' are particularly significant when discussing the findings of this chapter and the sustainability of food access in emergency systems: instability and inaccessibility.

Poppendieck (1998, pp.216–21) discussed the 'instability' of emergency food provision in the US on the basis of her findings in relation to the unpredictability of food supply, unreliability of financial support and dependence on volunteers. The former particularly chimes with the findings of this chapter, which highlight the instability of the food supply within these systems and the vulnerability of ongoing practice to changes in partnerships that provide much-needed financial and in-kind resources. Similarly, Poppendieck's (1998, pp.221–25) findings on 'inaccessibility' identify parallel issues of gaps in coverage, physical accessibility of projects, inconvenient opening times and discrepancy between the numbers of people in need and the numbers helped by projects.

The findings presented here on the sustainability of the food provided through emergency projects lead to three conclusions. In the first instance, the structures in which both actors examined in this chapter operate ultimately constrain their agency. The structure of the food industry – particularly the food retail industry – constrains the agency of emergency food organisations to make food available; the structure of emergency food systems – in terms of access procedures and ways of working – constrains the agency of people trying to access that food.

By right to food standards, the second conclusion is that the availability of food within these systems is not sustainable. This availability is vulnerable to the dynamics embedded in relationships with the food industry in terms of food sourcing, partnerships and future planning. To enable sustainable food sourcing, both case study organisations rely on retailers; FareShare to 'open up' surplus in their food chains, and the Trussell Trust Foodbank Network to open up their stores for nationwide access to food-donating consumers. To ensure the projects can continue to make the food they source available, partnerships are important ways of accessing funding and other in-kind support. Again, however, the nature of these can be shaped by partner organisations, with knock-on effects for how the providers work, and cannot necessarily be guaranteed into the future.

Such a conclusion points to a wider issue: the relationship between the sustainability of emergency food organisations and that of the wider food system of which they are part. This raises questions (beyond the scope of this research, but which could be pursued elsewhere) as to whether these emergency food organisations increase the sustainability of this wider food system through the role they play, or represent responses to that system's increasing unsustainability. They could, of course, represent both of these simultaneously; but when emergency food organisations are carrying increasing amounts of responsibility (as discussed in Chapters Six and Seven) for helping people in food insecurity and avoiding waste, it becomes even more important that focus also shifts to the dynamics and nature of the wider food system.

The third conclusion of this chapter is that, even when food is made available through these systems, access to it is not necessarily sustainable. Accessibility is not guaranteed to those who may be in need; it is constrained by both logistics and project processes, and is unprotected for those who do gain access. Eligibility criteria, referral processes and issues of physical accessibility can all limit people's agency in accessing emergency provision when they need to. But once there, the lack of rights recipients are afforded and the absence of accountability means their agency within these systems is also limited.

Therefore, both emergency food systems themselves and access to them could be said to be unsustainable on the basis of the analysis of agency presented here. Agency is highly curtailed by the systems in which it operates, with significant consequences for how this provision can be viewed in right to food terms. The lack of rights afforded to recipients and the level of vulnerability in these systems to not being able to source 'enough' food means these systems are extremely problematic when considered as a way of fulfilling the right to food when food insecurity occurs. This leads to the following key question, discussed in the next chapters and which centres around the idea of responsibility: who *should* be involved in respecting, protecting and fulfilling the right to food?

SIX

Food charity
as caring

As the first of two empirical chapters on respecting, protecting and fulfilling the human right to food, this chapter explores the role of emergency food charity in practice in its current form. Having examined the nature of and ways of working within the case study organisations (Chapters Four and Five), and given the absence of evaluative data, we need to know more about the aims and perceived achievements of emergency food providers from their own perspectives to better understand how their current practices (and potential future practices) fit within the context of protecting, respecting and fulfilling the right to food.

To better understand this emergency food provision in relation to the *problem* of food insecurity, the notion of 'need' is explored in the first instance; that is, what is need for this provision, and how does it relate to the experience of food insecurity? This chapter also explores the notion of success in emergency food provision, to come to a better understanding of how this provision might fit within the context of right to food *solutions*. It asks: what difference do these projects think they are making (in terms of success), and how does this relate to the right to food framework presented in this book?

This chapter also explores a more normative question about the role of charity in responding to the problem of food insecurity and realising the human right to food. It draws on the notion of responsibility to explore these issues. The ways in which these providers are, in practice, assuming responsibility for protecting against hunger is discussed, but a further question is raised: what role *should* these charities be playing? These questions set the scene for detailed discussion of the role of charity versus the state in Chapter Seven.

Care ethics is employed as a theoretical lens to guide the analysis. There is a rich literature exploring care and ethics; this framework is drawn on here in a particular way, adopting the term 'care ethics' to refer to 'a critical ethic of care and responsibility' (Lawson, 2007, p.2). Seeing care 'as a form of ethics' (Popke, 2006, p.506), the concept is drawn on to frame an understanding of care as social. As Williams (2001, p.478) described, care can provide a 'lens through which to make situated judgements about collective commitments and individual responsibilities'. While relational understandings of care and notions of interdependency are inherently embedded within such an interpretation, this broader conceptualisation allows for the possibility of examining care as something more; 'something which is being detached from broader, inclusive notions of the social through its commodification' (Green and Lawson, 2011, p.639).

Care ethics is chosen as the theoretical lens for this analysis for several key reasons. First, its emphasis on structure – the importance of structural-level caring and structural determinants of need for care – fits with the conceptualisations and definitions of food insecurity (structurally determined) and the right to food (realised through structural shifts and actors at all scales working together) engaged with in this book. Second (and particularly important for this chapter and Chapter Seven), the more recent care literature (Lawson, 2007; Williams, 2001) highlights the importance of neoliberal influences on how care is defined and put into practice (as increasingly privatised, individualised and marginalised). Third, as we will see here and as alluded to earlier (Chapter Four), the notion of caring is itself important to how emergency food providers understand what they do; the gesture and act of caring for those in need is at the forefront of their motivation.

Just as importantly, and particularly useful for developing an analytical framework, is the way in which care ethics takes account of the complexities involved in, and different scales at which, need is defined and care given. This is embedded within the idea that 'embodied caring practices must be analysed as multi-sited ... and as multi-scalar' (Lawson, 2007, p.6). This approach enables emphasis to be usefully placed on interactions between and within different scales (such as interpersonal, local, structural, long and short term) and sites (in the home, in the community, globally), many of which are present in or intersect with emergency food systems. This chapter reveals the ways in which this multi-sited care analysis facilitates an exploration of the complexities and tensions within and between the many sites embodied by emergency food provision.

Care ethics are used as a lens in two ways in the following analysis. In the first instance, care is seen as a practice that occurs at many different sites. Emergency food provision is explored as a practical response to food insecurity, embodied as a caring practice. This analysis allows us to appreciate how need, success and responsibility are multi-sited, and how ultimately emergency food provision is situated at only one or very few of the many sites that drive need, contribute to its relief or resolution and at which responsibility is held. On the other hand, care ethics provides the opportunity to explore the idea of responsibility in relation to the notion of care as social (not privatised or individualised), and to relate this to the right to food approach.

Need for emergency food

In the absence of systematic research and evaluation on the role and impact of emergency food providers, and in order to obtain a better idea of how this provision fits in relation to the experience of food insecurity, it becomes important to know more about what these organisations set out to achieve. A key factor for this is exploring who they aim to help – defined as in need of their provision. In turn, the way in which these projects define success has the potential to enlighten the role that these initiatives have – as a response to food insecurity, but most importantly in the realisation of the human right to food. This evidence is important for gaining a better understanding of how these organisations fit, in practice and in theory, within responses to the food insecurity 'problem' and the right to food 'solution'. In the absence of systematic research, political reaction and local policy response is premised on impressions of what these organisations do, based on the public information which is available. What this analysis enables is a much more critical exploration of exactly who these projects set out to help and how, which could in turn inform much more evidenced responses and expose those that are misinformed.

In terms of need for emergency food provision, the data collected provides evidence on both the organisational conceptualisation of need for emergency food and the procedures that established the practices of determining need. The findings illustrate that conceptualisations of need rely heavily on notions of crisis and immediacy, and both organisations apply procedures designed to independently establish that need.

External determinants of need

For both organisations, 'need' for emergency food provision is determined externally. FareShare's relationship is with the emergency food project itself rather than individual recipients of the food, so need is ultimately determined by those running the Community Food Members (CFMs). FareShare's CEO talked about their business model being based on the notion that the charities they supported with surplus food arose in response to local need; the existence of such a project is thus taken as a proxy for need. FareShare 'support[s] any organisation that is providing food as part of a safety net for people who are vulnerable' (FareShare CEO).

For the Trussell Trust Foodbank Network, the role of referrers is central to the model's approach to determining need. In order to obtain a food parcel, a voucher is required, which can be obtained from frontline professionals in the local community. It is therefore these professionals, who work with individuals (such as Sure Start Centres helping with early years support, or Citizens Advice Bureaus helping with debt/benefit support), who determine whether someone is in need of an emergency food parcel. The principle behind this system is that the professional will know something of the person's situation and will be helping them through their problems and circumstances (such as debt or access to benefits).

In both cases, therefore, the organisations procedurally distance themselves from the decision of determining need. In the case of Trussell Trust food banks, for example, this distance appears to be important in protecting project managers from the responsibility of determining the need of people whose circumstances they do not know; it also provides independent verification from someone who is familiar with a recipient's circumstances.

Internal notions of crisis and immediate need

However, both organisations conceptualise thresholds for determining the 'needy' through notions of crisis and immediacy. The Trussell Trust explicitly refers to provision for 'people in a short-term crisis' (Foodbank Network Manager). However, in practice it is unclear from the data how straightforward this threshold is – particularly in the changing economic context – and participants were aware of the complexity simultaneously embodied within and belied by discourses of crisis:

> Yes, we deal with immediate crises and so, yes, that is a basic premise of the food banks, but those crises arise as a consequence of a number of other factors. ... One of the growing ones is low income. That is not in isolation from the cost of living, the cost of fuel going up and wages being static. (Trussell Trust Wales Regional Development Officer (RDO))

For The Trussell Trust, this conceptualisation of need is also tied up with a particular faith motivation around 'feeding the hungry', as outlined in religious verse:

> 'I was hungry and you fed me, thirsty and you gave me a drink; I was a stranger and you received me in your homes, naked and you clothed me; I was sick and you took care of me, in prison and you visited me'. The righteous will then answer him, 'When, Lord, did we ever see you hungry and feed you, or thirsty and give you a drink? When did we ever see you a stranger and welcome you in our homes, or naked and clothe you? When did we ever see you sick or in prison visit you?' The King will reply, 'I tell you, whenever you did this for one of the least important of these members of my family, you did it for me.' (Matthew 25:35–40)

One interviewee – a trustee of a FareShare depot involved in a citywide initiative to coordinate emergency provision – also articulated this faith motivation to meet need:

> If I bring the faith element into it, you know, when I read my New Testament I read of a Jesus who, when approached by someone in need you know didn't say, 'well, that's all very well but let's talk about the longer-term issues here', you know, he met their need and in so doing he was then in a position to share something about life-changing issues and you know life-changing issues for individuals who are coming out of poverty can fundamentally be about you know the poverty bit, but there's also a sense in which there's some more transformational stuff that can happen and this isn't about proselytising, don't get me wrong, far from it, but from a faith perspective the more important thing is about recognising that people have need, being compassionate, getting alongside them and meeting their need with no real agenda other than to do that and if in the process of doing that you're sharing God's heart of love for a needy individual, family or community then great. (FareShare National Trustee and Trustee of FareShare South West)

There is something inherently practical in this faith-based driver, embodied in the very fact that such passages are seen to motivate social action. The way this interviewee talks about 'meeting need' in a practical way, of the importance of compassion as a gesture and experience, could all play a role in this conceptualisation of need and the meeting of it in an immediate, relational sense.

For FareShare, need is referred to as 'vulnerability'. As the earlier quote from the CEO demonstrated, food is distributed to projects working with 'people who are vulnerable'. The projects visited for this research (homeless accommodation, a homeless day centre, a homeless meal project and a refugee rights centre) all helped people who were particularly 'vulnerable' – so while the notion of vulnerability may be conceptualised broadly (to cover community cafes in deprived areas or lunch clubs for the elderly, for example), where the provision is an 'emergency' the populations helped are especially vulnerable and often experiencing acute crisis (for example, lack of housing or lack of citizenship status).

However, this data and previous research (Lambie, 2011) raises questions as to how far this notion of crisis is driven by project capacity and sustainability. As has been noted (and will be explored further in this chapter), these charities are highly professionalised; embedded within this professionalised and formalised approach is the notion of sustainability of the charitable models and protecting this into the future. Some food-bank managers made explicit reference to crisis being a 'doable concept' (Burngreave Foodbank Manager), or that they were not resourced for 'long-term food provision' (North Cotswold Foodbank). The notion of (avoiding) dependency is also invoked, with the crisis conceptualisation being a way of protecting this – but it is not necessarily clear if or how this links to sustainability: 'I think it's about crisis because I think, if you look at Lawrence Weston [an area of Bristol], most people are close to the breadline most of the time and we can't possibly solve that with a food bank because we'd make people dependent on something' (North West Bristol Foodbank Manager).

The 'three-voucher' policy at food banks – where someone can be given up to three vouchers in the first instance, and can only obtain a fourth when special arrangements are made between the referrer and food-bank manager – reinforces the fact that this is short-term, immediate help, not long-term support. This has been found to be connected in important ways with project sustainability (Lambie, 2011). However, supporting previous research (Lambie, 2011) this data found that the 'three-voucher rule' was not always adhered to and projects do support people on a longer-term basis. The existence of this cut-off process nonetheless provides projects with a system to fall back on if they are struggling with capacity.

From the findings presented here, it appears that organisational ethics to help the hungry, as well as vulnerability framing, could be determining the conceptualisation of need as urgent and immediate. On the other hand, project capacity and sustainability lead to a focus on what is achievable for the projects, in which context it makes sense to draw a line around this idea of immediacy.

Crisis, food poverty and wider lived experiences

The findings also reveal that, while conceptualisations of need for emergency food provision are seemingly bounded in terms of crisis or more extreme neediness, they are in fact located within projects' sensitivities of the drivers of this need and the complex underpinning experiences of poverty and low income. The care ethics approach to multi-sited and multi-scalar analyses is particularly important here to understand and account for this broader context.

Significantly, interviewees' definition of need as 'crisis' were discussed in interviews as part of a larger set of questions on the concept of 'food poverty'. This data revealed an awareness among participants of the relationship between the crises they were seeing in their projects and their recipients' wider circumstances of poverty. Interviewees talked about the need to address underlying causes of poverty. This very much fits alongside previous research, which highlights projects' own awareness of the limitations of emergency food provision as relief for the symptoms of food insecurity (Lambie-Mumford, 2013).

The Executive Chairman of The Trussell Trust also spoke in terms of precariousness and resilience. This provides a potential platform for situating the conceptualisation of need for emergency food as 'crisis' within the context of wider experiences of food poverty/insecurity:

> Because we are dealing with people whose ... elasticity is very, very limited, so you just move it £10 either way and people are in deep trouble.

> They don't have any resilience, they don't have any savings. (Trussell Trust Executive Chairman)

The small number of recipients interviewed also highlighted the importance of situating 'food crises' within the context of wider lived experiences. One was assessed as 'fit for work' and his benefit payments were not enough, another was roofless and the third was living in a sheltered housing scheme having fled domestic violence. These findings show the complex circumstances of emergency food recipients, and highlight the importance of looking beyond a food 'crisis' towards the underpinning drivers of that need.

This data demonstrates providers' awareness of the ways in which such crises embody wider experiences of poverty, precariousness, lack of financial resilience and complex household and income circumstances. Given these findings, it is possible to argue that projects actually see their definition of 'need' as crisis, within a wider context of vulnerability to these crises, informed by experiences of poverty. They therefore see need for their provision as part of (one site within) the food insecurity experience, which also incorporates mild and moderate experiences and sites of food insecurity. These findings therefore show that conceptualisations of need for emergency food provision are actually much subtler than they would appear when talked about in language such as 'crisis'.

However, the fact that the predominant language of crisis belies this subtlety could prove challenging to the progressive realisation of the human right to food in the future, should this language continue and these projects become the primary sources of support for people experiencing or vulnerable to food insecurity. There is a danger of this more restrictive framing rendering the underpinning drivers of this perception of need invisible. Tarasuk (2001) previously cautioned about the impact of food banks in framing these issues as a '*food* problem that can be addressed by giving food' (original emphasis, p. 489). In Canada, Tarasuk and Eakin (2005, p.184) also observed a dissociation between client need and food-giving rendering problems of unmet need invisible, providing little impetus for community groups or governments to find other solutions. So, while projects' understanding of the need they are seeing may be subtler and likened to a broader food insecurity conceptualisation, the ways in which need is understood in the wider discourse (as immediate and acute) could play its own role in how these projects are responded to, with emphasis placed on supporting charitable provision of food rather than on the underpinning drivers of need.

Success of emergency food projects

Previous research tells us that, from food security perspectives, emergency food projects have limited impact beyond the provision of food, but that where they are appropriate and tailored to recipients' needs they may help relieve symptoms of food insecurity (Lambie-Mumford et al. 2014). However, while helping people in crisis necessarily involves meeting immediate need, the successes and role of food-banks' caring practices also appear to be more complex and subtle.

The potential utility of the multi-sited and multi-scalar approach of care ethics for exploring the processes of caring through emergency food systems is significant, given that they involve food donors; referral agencies; volunteers; franchise projects, head offices and external partners – and are therefore inherently multi-sited. The analysis of notions of successful caring offered here shows how these projects are, in practice, multi-sited in the ways they care (as interpersonal exchanges of care, as projects providing safe spaces and as part of a wider welfare network) and situated at one of many scales on which care for people in food insecurity and poverty occurs.

Giving people hope and providing safe spaces

In the first instance, the data revealed a sense that caring was an end in itself and formed an important part of the success of emergency food provision. Food-bank provision was seen as giving people hope; for example, through being blessed with the provision and help received at a food bank, but also knowing that the assistance was there in the future. This suggests there is an interpersonal site of caring within this provision; that the relational experience of the gesture of care is significant in and of itself and has inherent value.

A clear finding from the data was that all kinds of emergency food projects (Trussell Trust Foodbanks and FareShare CFMs) were seen as providing places of safety; providing recipients with a safe and supported place was seen as key. Emergency food projects were also seen as important social spaces. Food banks offered spaces for recipients to talk to volunteers if they wished, and FareShare CFMs working with specific groups (such as homeless or asylum-seeking communities) saw the projects as providing safe social opportunities: 'it gives you a bit of hope, you know, that at least you've got somewhere, or you've got some people who can care a bit for you' (Emergency food recipient, Client 2).

Connecting to wider support

Importantly, some interviewees also saw the provision of food in response to crisis and to meet immediate need as forming a 'gateway' to other support. People access the CFMs or food banks to obtain help with food, but opportunities then arise for projects to work directly with people, and/or signpost them on for help with other issues they are facing that may relate to their need for emergency food.

Beyond the provision of food parcels and social interaction, the projects were seen as having a wider role in offering other direct support (particularly FareShare CFMs, such as homeless day centres), and/or as procedurally and metaphorically situated within a wider network of support (through the relationship between food banks and referral agencies, and food-bank signposting processes). For some FareShare CFMs that are not food banks, providing food is only one aspect of their work. Projects visited for this research included a homeless day centre (providing health services, training and facilities to vulnerably housed people in the city), a housing project (with a supported work scheme) and a refugee rights project (providing advice, computer training and other support). In such examples, food is just one of many different dimensions to projects' work, and is contextualised within access to other forms of support.

While this is not the case for food banks, the data highlighted that even these projects do not work in isolation, but rather are situated within the context of wider support. There appear to be two key mechanisms for this. The first is the relationship between the food bank and the referrer; the premise of the food-bank voucher is that it is issued while the referrer helps overcome the 'crisis'. The three-voucher rule provides food banks with a tool for returning to referrers to check on the progress of this support. Second, signposting provides food banks with a tool for moving people on to other services in the local community that may be able to help them with other aspects of support, identified during a recipients' visit. This signposting procedure has the potential to embed food banks within wider local support systems, rather than acting as isolated sites of support.

Findings on the importance of projects providing safe spaces and working as active parts of a wider welfare network suggest that, within the context of emergency food provision, caring operates at project and wider welfare network sites (in addition to the interpersonal site). In turn, this wider support and notion of connecting recipients to other parts of the welfare network helps us to understand where these projects fit in scales of caring. It shows that this form of multi-sited caring sits at one specific scale among many at which people in poverty and food insecurity receive care – from the household, social networks, the locality and national government.

Sites and scales of need and success

These findings suggest that emergency food projects may play a more complex role than is first apparent. While food security outcomes from the food on offer and the mechanisms for obtaining it may be limited, emergency food providers may play a more important social role: as spaces of care and facilitators of social support and welfare networks. This fits with the right to food approach, and is driven by not only the impetus to solve the problem of food insecurity but also the recognition that more is required, more issues and actors are involved and there are wider drivers of poverty at work.

The findings presented earlier in relation to notions of need for, and success of, emergency food provision show that those involved see the wider complexities of food insecurity beyond the notion of crisis, and recognise the need for and role of wider solutions. The multi-sited analysis of care used here enables this to be articulated and provides the opportunity to situate these interpretations within the complex contexts of drivers of need and broader solutions in which they fit.

We can therefore see how definitions of need and success are situated at one site – or very few sites – of the experience of, and responses to, food insecurity. Food insecurity and acute food crises represent a set of lived experiences and structural determinants that can interact with a range of support services. Importantly, those involved in this provision appear to be aware of these subtleties and complexities; the data suggests they are conscious of the broader picture of vulnerability, and consciously (in theory and practice) situate their provision within a wider network of support. Similarly, while the conceptualisation of need distinguishes a 'food crisis' from wider experiences of (lesser) food insecurity, the ways in which people involved in emergency food provision set out its impact (working at individual, project and wider welfare levels) indicate that they approach their work as part of a bigger picture of food insecurity and poverty.

Responsibility for care

Care ethics frames care as public, and therefore pushes back against neoliberal processes of the privatisation of care: 'Care ethics foregrounds the centrality and public character of care activities and so reframe responsibility. This reframing involves challenging neoliberal market logics that intensify the marginalisation of care by expressing (seemingly) everything in terms of personal responsibility or competition between communities' (Lawson, 2007, p.5). Care ethics therefore allows us to explore dynamics of the privatisation of care (in the form of support for food insecurity moving into the charitable sector) within the context of a social ethic, which sees care as structural and public. The notion of responsibility – who is responsible for care? – underpins this approach, and is the driving question of this section.

When looking at who is responsible for caring for those experiencing food insecurity and for working towards the right to food, two elements become particularly important: first, who is caring *in practice*; second, a normative question of who *should* care – and *how*. This part of the chapter first explores how emergency food charities are assuming the responsibility for alleviating experiences of food insecurity in practice, and how they are doing so in particularly streamlined and professionalised ways. The second part explores the structural interpretation of care, and highlights how complexity is actually embedded; that while responsibility should lie with the state and other structural-level actors, in fact emergency food providers try – in various ways – to navigate the scales between individual need and structural determinants.

Food charities as agents of care

In terms of who is taking responsibility for caring for those in food insecurity in practice, the data appears to suggest that emergency food providers are responsively assuming this responsibility as need grows and the welfare state retrenches. Interviewees talked about organisational growth as a response to demand (either for food banks or the availability of surplus for redistribution). However, providers' feelings about assuming this responsibility are not clear cut. The question of there being an opportunity – in terms of a renewed role for the church in social action – appears to be supported to some extent by the data, which highlights how food banks provide churches interested in social action with achievable projects. Some participants suggested an awakening to the importance of social action within the church over recent years, and that food banks can provide a sense of purpose when previously churches did not know what social action to get involved in. However, while some interviewees saw the pulling back of the welfare state and the 'stepping up' of the church into this type of provision as an opportunity for the church, others did not; instead, they saw it regretfully as a 'duty' of the church.

Food banks and the third sector: streamlined and professionalised

While those involved in provision may be conflicted about the perceived necessity of emergency food organisations taking this responsibility, they are doing so in practice regardless, and in particular ways. Both case study organisations are streamlined and have developed a range of professionalised processes to respond to perceived need and to assume responsibility in practice.

The Trussell Trust operates a not-for-profit franchise model. Franchisees pay an upfront franchise fee and are then required to work in particular ways and be audited annually; in return, they can use Trussell Trust branding and obtain training and ongoing support from regional and national level staff. FareShare operates a similar model; depots are encouraged to be independently viable social enterprises, which have to comply with food safety regulations and benefit from branding, training and – crucially – connections to food supplies, which are facilitated nationally.

While interviewees talked about organisational growth as a response to demand (either for food banks or the availability of surplus for redistribution), both organisations approached the practical realisation of this growth strategically. The Trussell Trust was considering logistical elements to facilitate its continued expansion, with the possibility for hubs where food is stored and from which individual food banks draw down supplies. FareShare sought growth through a process of building organisational reputation, so that the food industry would feel confident working with them.

The data revealed strategic visions for either a Trussell Trust Foodbank in every community or a FareShare depot servicing every part of the UK. It was further suggested that the two organisations, working together as the two biggest food charities in the country, could 'create a nation where no one need go hungry' (Trussell Trust interviewee). The growth of these organisations and this planned future trajectory was spoken of as a response to need; however, one strategic interviewee highlighted how some of this need was unnecessary, and could be overcome through resolving administrative mistakes and slow benefits systems.

The nature of these charities as highly professionalised, streamlined organisations could be seen as a result of an aspect of the market logic that Lawson (2007, p.5) identified: welfare diversification (see also Lambie-Mumford, 2013). An agenda pursued by New Labour governments (1997–2010) as part of the so-called 'third way' – now wrapped up in the Conservatives' 'Big Society' and welfare reform agendas – this diversification has involved the increasing involvement of the third sector in welfare provision, and a resulting professionalisation in the system as it has to compete (Alcock, 2010).

It could be argued, then, that these national emergency food organisations are charities of their time – a product of the changing landscape of the third sector over the last 17 years. Importantly, however (and as will be explored further in Chapter Seven), these charities are not taking on delivery contracts to form part of the formalised welfare system; rather, they are working in a vacuum left by formalised provision. As such, it could further be argued that while this is a new dynamic, it is nonetheless a by-product of this diversification. While we have always had food assistance, this provision is on a new scale and more formalised than before, and appears to represent a privatisation of care for the hungry: a shift from state-based responses to charity. Importantly, it is also occurring in the context of increasingly prominent discourses of personal responsibility for poverty, as well as welfare retrenchment.

These increasingly streamlined charities with national profiles are therefore seemingly taking responsibility for food insecurity where the state is not, for something the state is increasingly branding a problem of personal responsibility. This appears to be moving the discursive and practical work of helping people with acute experiences of food insecurity into the charitable sector.

Who should care for the hungry?

When looking at the question of who *should* care for those in food insecurity, this privatisation of care is counter to care ethics approaches, which advocate structural responses to caring and the public nature of care. Lawson's (2007, p.5) argument that care ethics can be used to understand care as structural and long-term finds affinity with the right to food approach's inherently structural interpretation of responsibility for preventing and protecting against food insecurity. This assumption of responsibility by charitable (private) initiatives is therefore in tension with a care ethics approach, which advocates care's public and central nature (for example, through state social protection) over privatised approaches (Lawson, 2007).

Political engagement and collective voice

However, once again complexity surrounds this analysis. The Trussell Trust in particular is negotiating the space between its experiences in local communities and wider structures, which are determining the need they are seeing. This suggests that – once again – multi-sited and multi-structural approaches to analysis might be helpful, to explore how privatised responses could influence the structural responses called for by care ethics and the right to food. In particular, the findings suggest that food banks and those associated with them have two key mechanisms at their disposal for negotiating the increasingly contested space between the demand seen in local communities and the policies and processes determining it: active political engagement (through advocacy, publication of data and shaping systems); and the power and influence of the collective voice of the church.

From the strategic Trussell Trust interviewees' perspectives, there are several important aspects to political engagement. First, as the network has grown, the Trust has increasingly become a 'voice for the voiceless' and has worked to change perceptions by providing information on who is 'going hungry'. While its primary focus remains the social action of providing food parcels, its campaigning work has become increasingly important; some in the Trust identify this as an aspect of their responsibility to make their information available and the voices of the people they help heard. Second, the Trust works to bring attention to the issues that their food banks identify; for example, problems with local Social Fund arrangements and problems with JobCentres not issuing short-term benefit advances and unfair sanctioning. However, there is a clear tension for the Trust in their approach to remaining apolitical; strategic interviewees talked at length about the ways in which their interjections related to processes, procedures and the implementation of policies, rather than the policies themselves:

> The ideal scenario is that we become a voice for those people. That is what we would want to do. The difficulty is that The Trussell Trust is and wants to remain apolitical. We want to stay out of the political sphere and not take one side or the other. (Trussell Trust Operations Director)

This apolitical stance is clearly problematic – and likely to become increasingly difficult in the context of further planned cuts to social security, given the politicised nature of food insecurity and food banks.

Beyond social action, however, other church voices are joining the wider debate and playing a considerable role in navigating this space between food-banks' work on the ground and the social security (welfare) system. The work of particular Christian non-governmental organisations, notably Church Action on Poverty, is particularly important here (Cooper and Dumpleton, 2013; End Hunger Fast, n.d.; End Hunger UK, n.d.). Several Christian bishops also recently wrote a letter to a national newspaper, calling for political attention to the issue of rising demand for food banks and the connections to 'cutbacks to and failures in the benefits system' (Beattie, 2014).

So, while emergency food provision may pose a significant challenge to structural interpretations of care, the data presented here indicates this is not a simple assertion. Projects are actively navigating between their 'privatised' and 'marginalised' work, and influencing wider structures that determine the experience of food insecurity.

Conclusion

The findings presented in this chapter highlight the complexity involved in understanding the need for and success of emergency food provision, as well as interpreting where responsibilities lie for preventing and protecting against food insecurity. The analysis shows that multi-sited approaches can help us come to a better understanding of how these projects fit within the lived experience of food insecurity (incorporating mild and moderate scales) – and the wider set of responses and welfare networks that could be said to help overcome it – in a right to food context (not just food, welfare rights, debt advice and so on).

It appears from this chapter that multi-sited analyses of caring practices could usefully inform future research on, and structural responses to, emergency food provision. They could do this by providing an analytical tool to account for the underpinning drivers of 'crisis' needs, the different levels at which emergency projects impact on those they help and the relationship between emergency food projects and wider welfare structures.

Importantly, the findings presented here highlight how 'need', 'success' and 'responsibility' – in relation to food insecurity and the right to food – are all multi-sited (in and of themselves, as well as in terms of how they fit with emergency food provision and the right to food). Furthermore, through a multi-sited analysis it becomes clear that emergency food provision can be seen as situated on one or very few of many different sites of need (relating to the wider experience of food insecurity), successful care (for the poor in the context of welfare systems) and responsibility (for caring and realising the right to food).

The first conclusion of this chapter is that need for emergency food provision – as presented by the interview respondents – can be situated as a crisis point within the context of the wider experience of food insecurity, in a way that takes account of not only scales of vulnerability and experience (mild, moderate or acute) but also the different sites that form the determinants of this experience. The notion of 'crisis' need, which is often presented, can therefore more effectively be placed in a wider context of structural determinants of food insecurity, financial insecurity and less severe food insecurity.

The second conclusion of this chapter is that, while emergency food provision is often talked about in terms of its limited impact on improving food security (providing relief from symptoms of food insecurity), the question of 'success' could be situated within the context of the range of sites and levels at which support for food insecurity and poverty occur. In practice, these projects' caring appears to operate at numerous sites: the individual level (through the act of caring); the project level (in terms of other services on offer); and in the context of the wider social support network (through signposting and referrals). Furthermore, the analysis presented here has shown how the nature of these initiatives can itself be situated at one site or level among many in which support operates.

In terms of responsibility, a third conclusion of this chapter is that emergency food organisations are assuming responsibility for caring for those in acute food insecurity where the state is not. However, the findings also show the particular ways in which these organisations appear to be navigating the contested space between individual need and its structural determinants– through campaigning and collective voice. In these ways, there may be opportunities for these organisations to hold others to account in the pursuit of the realisation of the human right to food.

Finally, care ethics provides an important tool, which will be particularly important in the next chapter for exploring the relationship between emergency food provision and the welfare state. Care ethics highlight the importance of social and structural caring – that care should not be relinquished by society in favour of ad hoc and marginalised charitable responses, in the context of prevailing rhetoric about 'deserving' and 'undeserving' people and increasingly personalised interpretations of poverty.

SEVEN

Food charity and the changing welfare state

The focus of this chapter is the role of the state in respecting, protecting and fulfilling the human right to food. Building on the work in Chapter Six on the role of charities, the role of the state is explored through the lens of social protection, specifically the ways in which state-provided social protection, through a welfare state, impacts on food insecurity and interacts with the rise of emergency food provision. The particular focus here is on the relationship between the changing welfare state in the UK and the rise of emergency food provision in the form of food banks. Social protection can be provided through civil society- or state-based organisations, and emergency food provision could be seen to represent an example of civil society-based protection. While De Schutter (2013, p.4) highlights the importance of informal, community-based social protection, from a right to food perspective the state is seen as the ultimate duty bearer for ensuring the right is protected, respected and fulfilled for all. Within a right to food context, universality, rights and entitlements are also important, particularly in relation to the fulfilment of the right to food when people are unable to access food for themselves. Food charity, then, insofar as it is neither universal nor an entitlement, poses a challenge to the right to food approach. This chapter explores the relationship between the formal welfare state in the UK and the rise of emergency food provision, and looks in particular at how changes to the welfare state are impacting on both the need for and shape of this ad-hoc charitable provision.

State-managed social protection takes many forms, and includes pensions and labour market policy as well as parts of healthcare. However, this chapter specifically examines aspects of the welfare state that protect people from poverty; namely, social security and services providing assistance to those in or at risk of poverty or out of work. It focuses on the relationship between these parts of the welfare state and the rise of emergency food provision as civil society-based social protection. This is a particularly important site for investigation, given the experiences of this relationship in other country contexts. In both the US and Canada, the numbers of emergency food projects and people turning to them for help grew in the context of economic recession and reforms to social security that introduced reductions in entitlements and a broader programme of welfare retrenchment (see Poppendieck, 1998; Riches, 2002).

Welfare reform and the welfare state

The concept and definition of 'the welfare state' has been the subject of many debates and discussions in academic literature. Veit-Wilson (2000, p.11) summarises its defining characteristics as 'policies to prevent poverty arising for anyone as well as those providing relief for such poverty as occurs'. Such a characterisation highlights the importance of the lens of responsibility to any study of a welfare state; that is, the responsibility a state claims for prevention of and protection against poverty. It also highlights the importance of distinguishing between social security (as a policy providing relief) and wider policies, which may incorporate a broader range of actors, to prevent poverty occurring (for example, by increasing labour market demand, minimum pay and benefit rates to adequate levels).Policies to reform social security entitlements (in terms of reductions and/or conditionality) and the need for and shape of food banking in the UK are emphasised here; the key reforms and policies are outlined in the following section. It is important to distinguish such welfare reform from the other side of recent cuts, which have seen reductions in finance to public services that also make up significant elements of the welfare state. The impact of these cuts to services has been discussed previously (Lambie, 2011; Lambie-Mumford, 2013) in relation to how budget cuts within services (such as social and probation services) led to professionals giving out food-bank vouchers, whereas previously they had discretionary budgets or other forms of support to help people through a crisis period. The emphasis on the notion of responsibility also raises an important set of questions relating to what responsibility the state is assuming, and will assume in the future, in the context of these reforms. It could be argued that key shifts in responsibility are embedded within the simultaneous proliferation of and reliance on food charity, and stringent and wide-ranging cuts to social security and services.

Welfare reform, austerity and food-bank usage

As we have seen, the growth in numbers visiting Trussell Trust food banks rose particularly sharply between the years 2012–13 and 2013–14, but overall significantly since 2010 (when 20 food banks were open). This growth occurred at the same time as the Conservative–Liberal

Democrat Coalition government initiated an extensive programme of reform to welfare policy in the UK, including to housing benefit, council tax benefit, child benefits and tax credits (Beatty and Fothergill, 2013; Taylor-Gooby and Stoker, 2011). In April 2013, a raft of these changes were introduced, including capping levels of income assistance that can be claimed through housing benefit and a reduction in the annual uprating of most working-age benefits. The role that welfare reform in particular is playing in demand for food assistance is a high-profile question in social policy commentary (Butler, 2014a; Daily Record, 2014). Within this context, food banks are cited across the ideological divide – on the one hand, celebrated as a communitarian response in the context of individualised risk; on the other, as a symbol of the failure of the welfare system (Gregory, 2014; Hanson, 2013). Parliamentarians and non-governmental organisations (such as Church Action on Poverty and Oxfam) are also engaged with this question, which was further explored during the Parliamentary Inquiry into Hunger and Food Poverty in Britain (Food Poverty Inquiry, 2014b; Perry et al., 2014).

These wide-ranging reforms take place in the context of a recent era of welfare austerity in the UK, which arose out of the economic crash of the mid-2000s and the recession that followed. They also fit into a wider historical trajectory of shifts in the shape and nature of the welfare state since the 1970s – and particularly since the beginning of the New Labour years in 1997, which saw the increased and changed role of the voluntary sector in welfare services, through programmes of diversification and a consequently more formalised and professionalised voluntary sector.

Welfare austerity: inevitability and significance

Since the economic crash, we have seen a programme of extensive cuts to services that form part of the welfare state and widespread reforms to social security; what some have termed an 'age of welfare austerity' (Farnsworth, 2011, p.251). This welfare austerity is discussed in a specific way as inevitable cuts in public spending. The Conservative Party-led Coalition government, on their election in 2010, prescribed austerity as the inevitable way forward on the grounds of 'unaffordability' (Blackburn, 2013; Kirkup, 2013). Yet, while austerity is framed as inevitable by politicians (Farnsworth and Irving, 2011), researchers have shown this is far from the case. From a political economy perspective, Hay (2005, p.198) showed how, while cuts to welfare spending are increasingly framed as an issue of economic competitiveness and a requirement of globalisation, empirical evidence across the Organisation for Economic Co-operation and Development countries shows this not to be the case and politicians retain much more autonomy in these shifts 'than they would like to acknowledge'.

This raises questions for how we can examine approaches to deficit reduction: as political and economic choices that are ideologically driven. For example, welfare austerity effectively constitutes a focus on cutting public spending to overcome government deficit, rather than a raising of progressive taxes (Farnsworth, 2011). This approach to balancing the budget can be seen as inherently ideological, driven by neoliberal notions of individual responsibility for risk, paternalism and communitarianism. Political rhetoric therefore serves to mask the ideology that drives it, presenting it instead as 'inevitable, unquestionable and un-ideological' (Farnsworth, 2011, p.259).

The data collected indicates that several reforms are particularly important. This section will briefly talk through each: the abolition of the Social Fund; the introduction of the 'bedroom tax' and changes to council tax benefit; increased length of sanctions; changes to criteria for Employment Support Allowance (ESA); and caps to entitlement and uprating levels. The Welfare Reform Act 2012 prescribed the abolition of the discretionary Social Fund, which covered crisis loans, community care grants and budgeting loans. Importantly for this study, crisis loans and community care grants were replaced by a twofold system:

'Payments on account of benefit' from the Department for Work and Pensions. These are 'short-term advances' (loans) to benefit claimants in financial need waiting for an initial payment or an increase in their entitlement. Payments on account in the form of 'budgeting advances' will also be available to claimants in receipt of Universal Credit as a replacement for Social Fund budgeting loans.

The second is local welfare provision provided by local authorities and the devolved administrations. (Simmons, 2013)

The Local Government Association (2014) reported that national funding for local welfare assistance schemes was cut from 2015. In the 2015 Local Government Finance Settlement, central government promised £74 million for upper-tier authorities, down from £172 million of funding the year before (LGA, 2015). Among a range of changes to housing benefit, the so called 'bedroom tax' relates to notions of under-occupation (see Beatty and Fothergill, 2013). Under the new rules, a three-bedroom family home (for example) would be ruled as 'under-occupied' if two children of the same sex under the age of 16 lived there, or two children of different sexes under the age of 10. Where a home is deemed under-occupied, the tenant loses '14% of their Housing benefit for one extra bedroom and 25% for two or more extra bedrooms' (DWP, 2012). An early evaluation of the policy change highlighted that 11.1% of social tenancies were affected by the policy and that 59% of those people were in arrears (had not managed to pay the full shortfall) (Clarke et al, 2014). Changes to council tax were also introduced in April 2013; where before the nationally administered council-tax benefit would pay up to 100% of a person's council tax, this was replaced by localised schemes (local council-tax support), which require minimum contributions that can vary by local authority and population group (Ollerenshaw, 2016). Support for people who are too ill to work (previously called Incapacity Benefit) has been replaced by ESA. Significant conditionality is embedded in this benefit, which involves 'more stringent medical tests, greater conditionality and time limiting of non-means tested entitlement for all but the most severely ill or disabled' (Beatty and Fothergill, 2013, p.5).

There have also been key changes to sanctions for out-of-work social security payments. In October 2012, the length of sanctions for Jobseeker's Allowance (JSA) recipients were increased. Under categories of 'higher, intermediate and lower', 'depending on the nature of the offence' (DWP, 2014a) people are sanctioned for 4–156 weeks for JSA or 1–4 weeks for ESA (DWP, 2013). In April 2013, a cap to the total amount of benefits out-of-work people can receive was introduced. No family of working age could receive more than £500 per week, and no single adult more than £350 per week. In November 2014 the DWP reported that over 51,000 households have been capped since it was introduced in April 2013 (DWP, 2014b). From 2016/17 this cap was reduced further to £23,000 per year in London and £20,000 a year elsewhere (Turner and Keen, 2015). A new system of uprating was also introduced (see Church Urban Fund, 2013 for a guide to this). Prior to April 2011, social security levels increased in line with the Retail Price Index; from April 2011, they instead increased in line with the (slower to rise) Consumer Price Index. This uprating policy was changed again in 2013, to rise by 1% per year for the following 3 years and from the years 2016/17 to 2019/20 most working-age benefits will be frozen (Turner and Keen, 2015). Given how recent many of these changes are, their cumulative consequences are difficult to ascertain – although evidence is emerging. Annual minimum income standards research shows that out-of-work benefits now provide even less of the income needed to achieve a minimum standard of living than they did in 2012. When taking into account the changes and rising cost of living, out-of-work benefits now account for 38% of the income a single working-age adult requires for a minimum socially acceptable standard of living (down from 40% in 2012), 58% for a couple with two children (down from 60% in 2012) and 57% for a single parent with one child (down from 59%) (Davis et al., 2012; Hirsch, 2013).

Food banks and the welfare state: the relationship

Given the ongoing governmental drive for increasingly localised, voluntary sector-driven 'welfare', it is helpful to establish where food banks fit among the mix of state-driven poverty prevention and alleviation policies (the formal welfare state) and wider community-based support. There are several mechanisms by which Trussell Trust food banks demarcate the space between their projects and the 'welfare state', particularly by not entering into contractual service-level agreements, as well as maintaining discursive and practical distance through voucher systems and rhetoric. Having said this, elements of this demarcation are problematic, including drawing a line around when they are or are not filling gaps in the welfare state, accepting grant funding (particularly at local level) and close relationships with social security agencies. Trussell Trust employees view the organisation as distinct and separate from the welfare state:

> The Trussell Trust is about not providing another means of benefit. We are not there to take the place of the benefit system. This was set up as a safety net for people who fell through the system. That is all it was ever set up for. More and more, it is becoming a means for people who really are struggling in our community. (Trussell Trust Operations Director)

One way to establish whether food banks (or similar projects) are part of or separate from the welfare state is to investigate those organisations that enter into agreements to provide services on behalf of the state (through service level agreements, for example). The Trussell Trust takes this distinction particularly seriously, as outlined in a webpage entitled 'A response to inaccurate and misleading reports about The Trussell Trust' (Trussell Trust, n.d.b):

> The Trussell Trust has advised our food banks against entering into contractual service level agreements with local authorities and do not think food banks should become part of state welfare provision. Trussell Trust food banks are there for those who slip through the welfare net in order to prevent a crisis turning into disaster, not a replacement for the welfare state. (Trussell Trust, n.d.b)

On a local level, those running projects on the ground also value the distinctiveness of food banks from the welfare state:

> I can't ever envisage us ever being an arm of the social services and I don't think most of us want it and I certainly don't and so I wouldn't consider having sort of a contract with the local authority to deliver local authority services according to their terms and conditions I think that's a non-starter. (Burngreave Foodbank Manager)

It is beyond the scope of this research to know whether or not all food banks have taken this advice. Neither are reports of local authority grant funding (which is not the same as funding for contracted services) necessarily clear on the terms and conditions of this funding (BBC, 2014; Butler, 2012). While taking this stance could provide the Trussell Trust Foodbank Network with some tangible – formal – distance from the welfare state, the picture is likely to be more complex when we look at FareShare Community Food Members. It is likely – but again, beyond the scope of this research – that some of these projects (for example, homeless projects, dry houses or adult day centres) may be involved in contractual service agreements with local or even national governments (for example, to provide housing, mental health or addiction services), making the relationship between the emergency food they provide and the formal welfare state more discreet and possibly less clear-cut.

Beyond not entering into contractual agreements with government bodies, food banks (in particular) also distance themselves from the formal welfare state in other ways, both in practice and discursively. These include through using referral systems and through discussing helping those who have fallen through the 'gaps' in the welfare system. Procedurally, a referral system (Trussell Trust projects use vouchers) provides both a formal link to and distance from the welfare state. While they provide a connection to formal welfare services – such as early years support (through health visitors) or unemployment support (through JobCentres) – they also enable the decision-making process, and ultimate responsibility for the individual's welfare, to remain in the state welfare system. Professionals give food-bank vouchers while they work to 'solve' a person's problem; recipients are referred from the welfare state, but remain within it, through this voucher link (see Lambie, 2011). This system allows food banks to distance themselves from the responsibility of deciding who is and who is not in need of their provision (as discussed in Chapter Six) – the idea being that they therefore do not determine who is eligible for what, or retain any responsibility for the solution to individual problems.

However, these lines of distinction between food banks and the welfare state are increasingly hard to draw and problematic. For example, while it establishes a discursive distance – with food banks below the net, catching what comes through – a question exists in turn for how far food banks may be plugging those gaps, and in so doing becoming a more formalised (albeit not necessarily state-funded) part of the welfare state system. The same question could arguably be raised in relation to the voucher system: while food-bank vouchers are seen as an important addition to the toolkit of professionals, including within state-funded services (Lambie, 2011), how far does this incorporate and thereby become an *in-practice* part of those welfare services' provision?

Two further subtleties remain. As highlighted previously, the distinction between contractual funding agreements and one-off grant funding is emphasised in the context of this debate. However, the terms of those grants – exactly what outputs and outcomes are being funded – may be important to explore. The BBC (2014) has reported that one third of local councils have funded food banks in their areas, but the nature of this funding is not necessarily clear. At a devolved level, the Scottish government launched the Emergency Food Fund as part of the implementation of welfare reforms. This fund (totalling £500,000) aims to 'support projects which respond to immediate demands for emergency food aid and help to address the underlying causes of food poverty' (Scottish Government, 2014). It outlines: 'Grants will be given to projects that concentrate on preventing food crisis recurring, those that build connections between food aid providers, advice and support agencies and organisations working to promote healthy eating and reduce food waste' (Scottish Government, 2014).

Finally, the statement that food banks are 'not part of the welfare state' could also be meant to refer to the fact that they are not a formal part of social security. However, an interesting question is raised here (and discussed in the findings later) regarding the relationship between food banks and local welfare assistance schemes and between food banks and local Jobcentre Plus agencies (which provide access to social security payments). In 2010, an agreement was made that Jobcentre Plus agencies would hold Trussell Trust food-bank vouchers (Trussell Trust, 2010). This was revoked in 2013 (Butler, 2013) in favour of a less formal 'signposting' system (Butler, 2014b), but this relationship is interesting to discuss briefly. Its rationale was that vouchers could be handed out when there is a delay or some kind of issue meaning payments are not coming through or have been stopped. But what does using vouchers in such a way that they may become a routine aspect of social security administration mean *in practice*?

State funding, particularly in the form of contracts, appears to be portrayed as the key marker for in/out of the welfare state. However, the subtleties highlighted show that – even if this is the case, and food banks and other emergency food charity are seen as part of a wider network of social welfare – how these projects may in practice be used as part of state provision (particularly in the giving and receipt of vouchers in statutory services) makes the line harder to draw.

The impact of welfare reform

This section presents findings on the impact of recent changes to welfare policy on demand for emergency food assistance, and the shape of these organisations as they respond to growing demand. It presents empirical findings indicating that both changes to the levels of social security entitlements and problematic welfare processes are impacting on needs.

Changing entitlements

The data collected indicates that changes to entitlements may be impacting on need for food charity by leaving people worse off. The findings highlight the impact of reforms that are reducing household incomes, such as the so-called 'bedroom tax', changes to council tax benefits and extended sanction lengths. Providers viewed the abolition of the discretionary Social Fund and its replacement with short-term benefit advances and local welfare assistance (managed by local authorities) as particularly problematic. Social security processes in administering welfare payments were also found to be problematic where they were leaving people without an income. This included inappropriate sanctioning decisions and errors made in declaring people on ESA fit for work – as well as more generally ineffective administration of welfare payments, which were sometimes delayed or stopped, leaving people with no or heavily reduced income. The findings relating to organisational change indicate that it has been a time of adaptation for food banks and the Trussell Trust Network, which is in the process of exploring appropriate ways of working for increased demand.

Social security reform and administration

The findings suggest that particular care must be taken when discussing the different impacts of social security on the need for and shape of food banks. There appears to be a relationship not only between social security *reform* and food bank need but also between social security *administration* and food bank need. This indicates a need for clarity around the impact of current welfare reform (in terms of policies changing social security) on the one hand, and the impact of social security processes (how it is administered) that are not necessarily part of these reforms on the other. Changes to social security policies (the Social Fund, housing benefit, benefit cap and extending sanctions) represent a change in the nature of social security entitlements. Problems brought about by sanctioning decisions, payment delays or inaccurate fitness assessments relate to social security processes. Much of the commentary relating to the impact of welfare reform appears, in practice, to conflate – or at least not neatly distinguish between – reported procedural problems and problems directly resulting from specific policies.

Schedule of reforms

It is important here to revisit a key methodological caveat. In the fast-moving context of both welfare reform and food assistance growth, the fact that the interviews for this research were undertaken on or before September 2013 means the chapter is not able to assess the impact of more recent changes. Furthermore, some of the data was collected before changes were implemented in April 2013, and some in the subsequent 6 months. Where this has a bearing on the findings, it is outlined and accounted for. However, the analysis revealed that participants interviewed before the changes were particularly anxious about the impact of changes to the Social Fund and Universal Credit. During and immediately after the changes, participants continued to talk about the impact of problems associated with the Social Fund (Universal Credit had not yet been fully rolled out) and other policy changes, such as the spare room subsidy change to housing benefit.

These findings are supported by claims made by The Trussell Trust nationally, as well as other research (Dowler and Lambie-Mumford, 2014; Sosenko et al., 2013; Trussell Trust, 2013).

The Social Fund

In terms of the ways in which changing entitlements may be affecting demand for food banks, devolution of the Social Fund was causing particular concern for the projects interviewed and impacting on the numbers of people being referred to food banks. A key concern was the huge variation in the ways in which local authorities were approaching the Social Fund, resulting in considerable confusion regarding what local people were entitled to and how they could access it: 'The thing that's really struck me is there's such a variety of different ways of dealing with the Social Fund through local authorities, it's exceptionally confusing and the way it was implemented wasn't very clear to anybody. It's left the third sector … overwhelmed' (Trussell Trust Foodbank Network Director).

Even more problematically from the food-banks' perspectives were local authority approaches to the provision of crisis loans, which in some way incorporated local food banks. In Bristol, for example, at the time of the interviews the council was consulting on a proposal to give people a one-off payment card per year, and thereafter referring them to local food banks. The potential implications of co-opting food banks into these support systems were clearly a concern for participants involved in food banks, many of whom were actively resisting:

> I was sitting in a meeting the other week and I was told … if we have a one-off payment card for people here, the plan is that people can have one a year and then they'll be referred to food banks by whatever agency takes this over and my answer to that was 'you are assuming that we are going to take on your agency as a referral agency' and I said 'I'm not going to guarantee that'. (East Bristol Foodbank Manager)

Approaches to the Social Fund also vary by devolved nations. It is important to note that this data was from English food banks, and different systems are in operation in Scotland, Wales and Northern Ireland.

Reduced entitlements and increased conditionality

In September 2013 – 6 months after the implementation of key reforms to social security – strategic-level staff members also identified other policies they felt were contributing to increasing demand. In particular, they highlighted the cap to benefit payments, the spare room subsidy and tightening criteria for ESA, leading people to be moved from an illness-based allowance to income support:

> So those are three policies [spare room subsidy, tightened criteria of ESA and cap on uprating], which have driven up [need]. I'm not going to quote the stats because you've got them from us haven't you. 52% of people coming to food banks since April, are there because of benefit delay or benefit change, whereas it was 43% the year before, 20% 6 or 7 years ago. Food banks that have been around for years are seeing more and more people coming through. (Trussell Trust Executive Chairman)

These findings are supported by other research. For example, Dowler and Lambie-Mumford (2014) indicate that changes to council tax benefit and the spare room subsidy may be having particular impact on food-bank uptake, and delays in payment or problems caused by changing benefit type can cause financial difficulty. Since April 2013, The Trussell Trust have also reported they were providing a bigger proportion of parcels for problems relating to benefits than the same time in 2012 (Trussell Trust, 2013).

Administration of benefits

As well as changing entitlements, problematic processes or procedures were also found to be affecting demand for food banks. Decision making around sanctions were particularly problematic from food-banks' perspective, and decisions seen as unfair and/or arbitrary: 'We can be certain that those being sent to us with a sanction, it is, generally speaking, quite often a fairly unfair decision. Sometimes, I've got to say, a totally bizarre decision' (Trussell Trust Foodbank Network Director).

Furthermore, some project managers saw changes (introduced in October 2012) to maximum sanction length as problematic, given the financial insecurity that many living on social security are already in:

I think it's quite easy to tick the wrong thing on the phone or on the form and then you won't have any money and if you don't have any reserves you haven't got any money to buy food with. I think with sanctions being increased in length, this could be a more serious problem in the future. I mean if we're only going to give people three lots of food but they've been sanctioned for 6 months or something I'm not sure what they're going to do, I don't even know what the government expects them to do. (Burngreave Foodbank Manager)

These findings indicate two potential dimensions to the ways in which social security is affecting the need for emergency food, based around the distinction between reforms and administration. On the one hand, reforms are leading to changes to the level of entitlements people can receive, leaving them worse off with reductions in their real income. On the other, problematic processes – such as mistaken sanctions or fitness assessments and delays in payments – can mean people's incomes are heavily reduced (if they still receive a tax credit or other type of benefit), or stopped altogether.

Food banks: responding and adapting

Within the context of this growing demand for and provision of food banks, the data revealed how both individual food banks and the Trussell Trust Foodbank Network as a whole have responded and adapted. Previous research identified how the food-bank franchise model and its faith basis were key factors in the development of the first 148 food banks (Lambie, 2011). The localised approach and notion of helping a neighbour were also seen as important. Since 2011, individual food banks and the Trussell Trust Foodbank Network have become more established and are facing increasing demand. The data indicates this has resulted in changing ways of working locally and the emergence of identifiable local 'systems'. It has also resulted in changes in ways of working nationally for the Trussell Trust Foodbank Network, including an ongoing professionalisation and changes to processes and procedures, and a parallel reimagining of the nature and conceptualisation of the localised aspects of individual projects.

Sheffield and Bristol

The case study cities of Sheffield and Bristol highlighted the ways in which local relationships among individual projects were developing. In some ways, they provide contrasting examples. Bristol had a formalised 'charter', which many charities and local projects had signed, and carried a formal name: the Bristol 5K Partnership. The Partnership had a fairly logistical focus, working on collecting food across the city, leveraging funding and contemplating issues of food storage and transport:

> Over the last year we have been exploring how we can develop a more strategic approach to the way that we address the issue of food poverty and that's basically saying how can we work together in a way which is working with the council, working with other stakeholders, working with the food industry, working with FareShare, Foodbank Network, Matthew Tree Project, all of those organisations with an interest in food poverty, how can we plan and implement addressing the issues of food poverty in a more strategic way and we've done that under what we're now calling the Bristol 5K Partnership. (FareShare National Trustee and Trustee of FareShare South West)

In Sheffield, on the other hand, a looser network of food-bank projects had developed – referred to as the Sheffield Foodbank Network – which meet regularly on a relatively informal basis to share knowledge and experiences:

> I think it is important that we all know what we're doing. It's important for simple, logistical, reasons to make sure we're all, well one that we're not all feeding the same people, and that people aren't just going round from food bank to food bank to food bank; there's some kind of semblance of order to that. Secondly that there's some kind of semblance of understanding of some of these issues, so part of my role being there is to be a voice to some of these issues that I've raised and the fact that even if people don't agree with me, at least they've been said and at least they've been heard then. But I suppose I also see it, I think it is important also from a faith perspective to get this kind of like, a shared

understanding of what we're actually doing around this issue as a church. (Parsons Cross Initiative Manager)

Both groups of projects used these relationships to work through issues of geographical boundaries and clarify which food banks covered what areas of the cities. They had both interacted with their local councils and some local Members of Parliament. In both cities, there were queries over the aims and anticipated outcomes of these relationships – and, at times, feelings of ambivalence regarding meeting without clear aims in mind. Yet at the same time, in both cases some members were reluctant to formalise the networks. Such networks appear to provide opportunities for knowledge sharing and overcoming tensions – in particular, any conflicts surrounding supermarket collections or food drives, and (where independent and Trussell Trust projects sit at the same table) opportunities for managers to find ways to work together and establish geographical boundaries. While such coordination may be beneficial for learning and sharing good practice, they raise a question regarding the extent to which localised systems are emerging and becoming embedded.

National debates and action

At a national level, organisational change in the Trussell Trust Network appears to be underway – in terms of processes and procedures, and (relatedly) conceptualisations of the idea of a 'local' food bank. In terms of processes and procedures, an important new layer of management has emerged in The Trussell Trust in the shape of Regional Development Officers; there is now one such Officer for every region in England, two in Wales and a growing team in Scotland. The Trust also now employs a Partnership Co-ordinator in London, who brokers requests from businesses to support food banks in the city.

At the time of the interviews, the Trust was discussing whether it required a different way of thinking around the storage and distribution of donated food – with larger hubs storing the food and food banks withdrawing it – to reduce the costs and volunteer input required to run a food-bank project: 'There is a situation now where food banks, because of all the extra collections we are getting, are getting spikes of food that are really difficult to store. Rather than people having to take on more expensive rental storage, the hope is that we can put hubs in' (Trussell Trust Head of Fundraising). The data also indicates that the Trust was considering reconceptualising the way food banks were identified. At the time of writing, the Network counts the number of franchised food banks – but those food banks have distribution centres across their area, sometimes run by different volunteer groups. The question of whether these distribution centres should form the focus for understanding the scale of the work and identifying locality has been raised: 'People talk to me about "my food bank". They don't necessarily mean the food bank … But they mean the distribution centre that is in their part of town' (Trussell Trust Executive Chairman). This could be seen as a parallel question to that of larger storage hubs and distribution networks. Further, this re-conceptualisation of distribution centres could be a way of getting around some of the procedural and logistical issues to which the storage hubs are a response. A knock-on effect of this may be the Trussell Trust Foodbank Network becoming more identifiable as a food bank or food pantry system, with local food pantries withdrawing food from a centralised food hub (although one strategic interviewee referenced a system in which the food would be stored for the food banks that collected it, thereby maintaining the 'food for local people from local people' approach):

> But with logistics it's slightly different. We've said, and we're looking at the advice here. Principle, if you collect the food locally you want to promise somebody that it will go to local people. So if I get the food in Tower Hamlets and it disappears off to a big warehouse in Rugby, it needs to come back to Tower Hamlets. Now the logicians have said, 'No problem at all'. We do that all the time. 'It's binning'. Okay, that's fine. (Trussell Trust Executive Chairman)

This quote suggests that this conceptualisation may open up a different way of thinking about or retaining localism, where there is a national network, regional coordination and a city- or town-wide food bank but very localised operations in the handing out of food itself. Both this increasingly localised conception of distribution centres and the idea of larger food hubs allows for much greater capacity for food banks to become bigger and able to support more and more distribution centres.

Food banks therefore appear to be responding and adapting to growing demand in particular ways at various geographical levels: locally by working more closely together, and nationally by streamlining procedures and rethinking scales of food storage and its provision to accommodate the future trajectory of need.

Where next? The future relationship between food banks and the welfare state

The findings presented in this chapter highlight the symbiotic relationship between the withdrawal and retrenchment of the welfare state and the growth in the provision of and need for food banks. The consequence of this is that these projects – however unintentionally – risk becoming part of the welfare state, and actually enabling its further withdrawal.

We appear to have reached an important moment in food banking in the UK. While food banks currently appear to be doing their best to resist incorporation into social security processes, the relationship between locally run welfare and local food banks is particularly concerning. If these systems routinely refer people to food banks instead of providing financial support themselves, it is hard to see where the line can be drawn. And if funding is withdrawn altogether from this support – as has been reported (Local Government Association, 2014) – an urgent question emerges regarding the role food banks play in local communities. At a national level, food-bank demand appears to signal the inadequacy of both social security provision and the processes through which it is delivered. If these issues are not addressed, the point at which food banks become an extension (if not a formal part) of a failing welfare state might not be far away.

The framework presented at the beginning of this chapter located food banks as distinct charitable organisations, separate from 'the welfare state' – albeit in slightly problematic ways, with key caveats. But what are the implications of the impact of welfare reform and the future trajectory of further reform for this relationship? The notion of 'responsibility' – namely, the responsibility the state assumes for protecting against and preventing poverty – is important for exploring this question, and two potential eventualities are reflected upon here. First, food banks could become increasingly embedded parts of the welfare state, where the state maintains responsibility for alleviating poverty (through, for example, a continuation of local welfare assistance schemes). Alternatively – with an end to funding for local assistance schemes, reductions in social security entitlements and failures to rectify inadequate processes – food banks could remain distinct, non-government-funded initiatives, but ones that work in local communities in the absence of state responsibility for poverty alleviation.

The developing relationships between some food banks and local authorities and the nature of referral procedures – particularly relationships between the Department for Work and Pensions and food banks – raises the issue of how far food banks may in practice become *part of the welfare state*. While local authorities may not be establishing service-level agreements with food banks as part of their local welfare assistance schemes – and similarly, referral relationships between food banks and statutory bodies may not be formalised – the lines of distinction may become hard to draw if practices become embedded and localised systems of formal and informal support develop. However, in such an eventuality responsibility may still (to some extent) be held by the state, in the form of statutory organisations, local authorities and government departments.

On the other hand, food banks may remain distinct initiatives but find themselves *working in the absence of the state* taking responsibility for adequate protection against poverty (food charity assuming the responsibility for care is discussed in detail in Chapter Six). This possibility is raised by the potential abolition of local welfare assistance schemes, reductions in social security entitlements to even less adequate levels and failures to rectify inadequate procedures and processes. If the state provides no emergency assistance at local level when no other social security option is available, food banks and other charitable initiatives may become the only agencies taking responsibility for helping local people in need. Similarly, where reductions in social security entitlements (through extended sanctions, caps, changes to housing benefit and council tax benefit) leave people worse off and unable to afford even the most basic of diets, food banks may take responsibility for helping people who turn to them because they cannot feed themselves and their families.

There could be a third, slightly more subtle eventuality: through the voucher referral system, food banks may not necessarily become a distinct part of the system, but may effectively become enrolled within its delivery – providing, as they do, a 'tool' for statutory services to call on when tackling chronic need.

However things develop, local welfare assistance is likely to be key to determining the role of food banks if systems develop around them or the state provides nothing to replace funding.

Conclusion

Now is a dynamic time for social protection in the UK; there is ongoing change and discussion, driven by ideology and questions of who should be providing that kinds of services, who is best equipped to do so and what the best kind of support looks like. Overall, what is emerging is a leaner welfare state; this retrenchment is impacting on both the need for and shape of food banks. The rise in need for, and changing shape of, food banks and other food charity are ultimately representative of the wider shifts occurring in the era of welfare austerity. Indicators of rising need relate to policies of increasing conditionality; for example, where people need food vouchers because of long sanctions or having failed a fitness assessment for disability benefits. At the same time, food banks represent the individualisation of risk that has underpinned welfare austerity, with people left without adequate assistance from the state and forced to turn to charitable responses. This story of food charity could also be seen to embody the decreased role of the state in favour of community responses, in the context of increasing emphasis on individual and community-based responsibility.

While the rise of food banks could in practice symbolise the increasing responsibility held by civil society-based social protection, the right to food approach stipulates that the state is the duty bearer, and that everyone's right must be fulfilled when they cannot provide food for themselves. As such, any shift from entitlement to charity (which is neither a right nor accessible to all) is a particularly problematic aspect of the contemporary shift in food-based social protection. These findings appear to represent just that, indicating that levels of entitlements – and the administration processes that organise them – are neither adequate nor sufficiently streamlined to prevent food insecurity in the UK. Furthermore, the organisations responding to this are local-level community projects. Having said this, a right to food approach does not necessarily mean social protection is provided exclusively by the state, as duty bearer, in the form of welfare provision. It could involve other state interventions; for example, in the food market or labour market to ensure financial security or fairer access to affordable food. It could also mean that civil society organisations are involved in social protection in some way – so long as this was entitlement-based. Ultimately, the state is responsible for ensuring the right to food is adequately fulfilled – but what this fulfilment looks like in practice is open to discussion.

EIGHT

Conclusion

The empirical chapters of this book explored the acceptability and sustainability of emergency food systems in relation to the availability and accessibility of the food they provide (Chapters Four and Five), and the role of charity and the state in this provision and in relation to the right to food (Chapters Six and Seven). In doing so, these chapters explored emergency food provision as a system and the adequacy of that system in terms of its social acceptability and sustainability, as well as critically engaging with the role of charity in helping people to access food.

A large amount of data was collected through the duration of this study. This book has done its best to shed light on the wide range of insights and detail this data provided into the emergent and changing phenomenon of emergency food provision in the UK. Its system-level analysis and wider sociopolitical critique enabled the presentation of new findings about these systems, their relationship to wider social and political shifts and their future trajectories.

These findings reveal the complexity of emergency food systems in relation to the range of moral and ethical motivations and values that give meaning to the endeavour, from the perspective of those running these organisations and local projects. The analysis also highlights some of the tensions embedded within these systems in terms of the accessibility of the food to those in need. Framing the analysis with a sociopolitical critique enabled the book to explore how the emergence of these systems is intimately connected to shifts that open up space for this kind of provision – such as a retrenched welfare state and increasingly diversified safety nets – and link to wider political and discursive shifts that emphasise individualised responsibility and risk for poverty.

This concluding chapter discusses some of the key findings arising from these analyses, how they extend our knowledge of emergency food systems and their implications for how we might progressively realise the right to food in the UK. Guided by the theme of 'opportunities in crisis', the chapter emphasises the question of what can be *done* on the basis of the findings, and how the circumstances underpinning emergency food provision and the need for it may present a chance for more progressive ways forward. Emphasis is therefore placed on the implications of the findings, and how they can practically be responded to.

The chapter begins by discussing the implications of the key findings from each empirical chapter of the book. This is followed by a discussion of some of the key themes that cut across these chapters, and how the findings represent a considerable step forward in knowledge about emergency food provision in the UK. The particular 'opportunities' that can be identified within the context of 'crisis' are outlined, and the utility of the right to food approach for drawing conclusions is discussed.

Three key conclusions are then presented. The first relates to the need to challenge minimalist approaches to defining and responding to the problem of food insecurity. It is based on findings on the importance of socially acceptable food experiences, and the wider context of vulnerability and insecurity in which need for emergency food provision is situated. This conclusion calls for broad conceptualisations that take into account structural determinants of need for emergency food provision, the importance of social inclusion and responses that focus on enabling everyone to have socially acceptable, secure food experiences.

The second conclusion relates to the importance of rights-based policies to move us forward from the current situation, in which there is increasing reliance on emergency food provision in the context of a retrenched welfare state. Guidelines set out by DeSchutter (2010) are discussed in relation to practical next steps that could be taken to put the right to food into practice in the UK.

The third conclusion is that, given findings relating to the limitations of the food provision itself (compared to other relational and social contributions, by right to food standards), there could be a progressive social and political role for emergency food provision in realising the right to food. Such a role could entail organisations focusing on the individual- and local-level social care they provide and their political work through advocacy, campaigning and holding other actors to account.

The chapter concludes with some key recommendations, based on the book's findings. Recommendations are suggested for a range of stakeholders, including emergency food providers, policy makers, NGOs, the food industry, local communities and individuals, and researchers.

Advancing knowledge of emergency food provision in the UK

The findings presented in the Chapters Four to Seven have important implications for our knowledge of emergency food systems in the UK. The findings of Chapters Four and Five show that emergency food systems are ultimately neither adequate nor sustainable by right to food standards, which emphasise the importance of the social acceptability of food acquisition on the one hand and the sustainability of food access into the future on the other. They illustrate how emergency food provision forms an identifiably 'other' system to the socially accepted mode of food acquisition in the UK today; that is, the commercial food market through shopping (Chapter Four). They also show that providers are not necessarily able to make food available through these systems, with their ability to do so shaped in important ways by the structure of the food industry in which they operate (Chapter Five).

Importantly, when considering their potential role in creating progressive solutions to food insecurity and realising the right to food, emergency food systems are ultimately experienced as 'other' and associated with powerful 'othering' discourses (Chapter Four). This has important implications for the question of acceptability, given the experience and social construction of exclusion that the findings indicate. Furthermore, the findings highlight that people do not always have the ability to access emergency food projects and their food whenever they wish, for as long as they need (Chapter Four). This calls into question the systems' ability to provide systematic and dependable sources of food to all those in need.

The findings from Chapters Six and Seven indicate that the state is, if anything, retreating from its duty to respect, protect and fulfil the human right to food – and that emergency food provision is assuming the responsibility to fulfil this right, where it can and in its own way. It appears that emergency food provision is increasingly assuming responsibility for protecting against food insecurity (Chapter Six). These organisations are assuming this responsibility in parallel to the significant withdrawal of the welfare state (in the shape of cuts to services' funding and reductions in entitlements to social security). This is impacting on both the level and nature of need for emergency food, as well as the context of other welfare support in which these projects operate (Chapter Seven).

The findings of Chapters Six and Seven indicate that emergency food providers are responding in a professionalised manner and at a national scale. This is a product of welfare diversification over the last two decades, as well as the changing nature of the voluntary and community sector (VCS) (Chapters Six and Seven); but it also represents the marginalisation and privatisation of care (Chapter Six). These findings imply a symbiotic relationship between the rise of national-scale emergency food assistance charities, the retrenchment of the welfare state and the larger role an increasingly professionalised VCS sector is playing in the care of the poor in the UK.

Three key themes are identifiable from the empirical findings presented in this book. These have important implications for how the discussion of emergency food provision can move on and tangible responsive actions to it be developed.

Moral imperatives

The first theme relates to the way in which emergency food provision represents an important embodiment and performance of caring (Chapter Six) and morality (Chapter Four). Providers clearly and strongly stated the moral imperatives that motivated their work (to reduce waste and hunger) and described how their projects provided spaces in which acts of caring were performed and vulnerable people could be cared for. As an embodiment of these social and moral acts and motivations, emergency food provision can be celebrated. These organisations clearly provide the space and opportunity for people in local communities to express care for and generosity towards their neighbours, at a time when state provision is reducing and increasingly conditional.

Structural determinants

The second theme to emerge from the findings is the importance of structures in determining need for (Chapter Seven), access to and availability of food (Chapter Five) in emergency food systems. Building on the definition of food insecurity used in the research, which points to the importance of structures in determining the accessibility of food generally (for example income, retail and transport), the findings highlight the important role played by other structures (the welfare state, the food industry and emergency food systems themselves) in determining the nature of the provision and the experience of accessing it.

The structure of the welfare state was found to play an important role in both driving need for emergency food and (as a consequence) shaping the nature of projects (Chapter Seven). The availability of food within emergency food systems was influenced by the structure of the food industry; projects relied on retailers for access to consumers (to solicit donations) or surplus (from further down supply chains) (Chapter Five). The structure of emergency food systems themselves was also found to be significant in terms of determining access to the food they provided – particularly when projects required referrals, only opened a few times per week or imposed limits to the amount of help any one person could receive (Chapter Five).

This highlights the importance of taking structures into account when studying the emergency food phenomenon. Studying these projects in isolation would not reveal the important political and socioeconomic drivers of the need for and shape of emergency food provision, or the ways in which the systems themselves can constrain the agency of (potential) recipients.

Neoliberalism, welfare and care

The third and final theme to be extracted from the findings is that emergency food provision simultaneously represents an embodiment (Chapters Four and Six), consequence (Chapters Five and Seven) and contestation (Chapters Four and Six) of neoliberal processes in systems of food, welfare and caring. Shifts such as the retrenchment of the welfare state (in terms of social security provision), the changing nature of caring for people experiencing poverty (reductions in funding for state services; increasing emphasis on the VCS and local communities to respond) and a food system dominated by large retailers (which control pricing and dominate retail infrastructure) form important backdrops to the rise of emergency food provision. The findings highlight the complex and contradictory nature of the relationship between emergency food provision and these neoliberal dynamics.

In the first instance, the findings suggest that emergency food organisations form a protest against these shifts. Their embodiment of moral imperatives of reducing hunger and food waste – both identified as consequences of unjust (food, welfare and caring) systems – were apparent in the data (Chapter Four). Similarly, the ways in which these systems provided important spaces for caring – compared to less caring welfare systems, or in the absence of state care – were also apparent (Chapter Six).

Yet, this notion that emergency food systems are protests against neoliberalising shifts is contradicted by other findings, which suggest that these systems may not only exist as a *consequence* of these shifts but also *embody* them. The rise of emergency food provision could be said to be a *consequence* of such shifts, particularly in relation to how welfare retrenchment has driven need for the provision (Chapter Seven) and how interest from the food industry – driven by corporate social responsibility agendas – has resulted in access to surplus and privately donated food increasing exponentially in recent years. Conversely, emergency food providers could be said to *embody* neoliberalising shifts because they represent a privatised approach to care (Chapter Six) and an exclusion from mainstream food experiences involving commercial markets and shopping (Chapter Four).

Contributions of a systems-based analysis

The findings presented in this book represent a considerable step forward in our knowledge about emergency food provision in the UK. They provide the first systems-based analysis, and tell us that key social and market-based values are embedded within these systems – and are problematic from a human rights perspective. The findings also highlight the role that welfare politics – at the level of both service provision and social security – is having in driving the need for and shape of these initiatives. They also serve to advance our knowledge of emergency food systems by highlighting the vulnerability of people in food insecurity in relation to these systems as a result of their lack of agency to access this provision and the food therein.

The book's contribution to literature on emergency food provision in the UK is particularly apparent given the emergent nature of this phenomenon (Lambie-Mumford et al., 2014). Through applying and developing a right to food framework, the book and its findings contribute to a better understanding of food rights – and the role of emergency food provision in their realisation – in the UK, as well as providing a comparison with other countries in the Global North and the work of rights-focused researchers such as Riches (2011).

More broadly, the findings and theoretical developments presented in this book contribute to other areas of academic literature – particularly wider food and social policy research. In the first instance, the book contributes important evidence to the growing food studies literature of a new phenomenon in the UK food system; one that could be said to embody key failures of that system. In so doing, it could contribute to work on the nature of the commercial food systems itself, experiences of the commensality of food across different food experiences and studies of notions of 'alternative' food provisioning (see, for example, Jackson and Group, 2013; Kneafsey et al., 2008).

Second, the book provides key theoretical and empirical evidence relating to one particular consequence of the changing nature of the social contract in the UK. It makes a significant contribution to social policy research by providing detailed evidence on the symbiotic relationship between the growth of charitable emergency food provision and the retrenchment of the welfare state. Historically, the engagement of social policy research in the UK with the issue of food insecurity (or related concepts) – in isolation from studies of poverty generally – has been very limited (the work of Dowler, 2003, being an important exception). This research could help pave the way for social policy researchers in the UK to pay more attention to food insecurity and food charity in the future.

In applying care ethics (Lawson, 2007) to the study of emergency food provision, the book has also contributed to this particular literature. It has shown how care ethics can further advance our knowledge of complex and contradictory social phenomena that operate on and affect various sites and scales simultaneously. This theoretical approach also helps us to understand state-based provision – particularly social security and social services – and its importance as a public mode of caring. By employing theories of agency, the book has also emphasised the importance of theories of power when exploring the food system and access to it. It has shown that applying these theories to emergency food systems has been particularly insightful when related to the work of Poppendieck (1998) and Tarasuk and Eakin (2005).

Opportunities in crisis: towards conclusions

In the context of the evidence presented in this book (and elsewhere in related studies of contemporary experiences of poverty), as ad hoc charitable organisations assume responsibility for those in acute food insecurity in the context of a reduced welfare state, ongoing austerity and rising costs of living – what can be *done*? The remainder of this chapter is framed by the notion of opportunities in the context of crisis. It explores how we can draw on the charitable provision that has emerged, and responses and reactions to it, to identify more progressive ways forward.

Potential opportunities reside in the current shape, scale and nature of reaction to emergency food provision and food insecurity in the UK. First, the scale of participation in these systems – in terms of numbers of people volunteering and donating food – indicates the extent of public concern regarding food insecurity. In 2015–16, the Trussell Trust Foodbank Network reported that approximately 40,000 people volunteered at food banks across the country, and that members of the public donated 10,573 tonnes of food (Trussell Trust, n.d.a).

Second, the range of organisations involved in emergency food provision suggests that the wider VCS is also mobilised by the issue of food insecurity. Multiple faith groups – including various denominations of Christian churches – are involved in food-bank provision, and a range of initiatives hold food-bank vouchers in local communities. While driven by corporate social responsibility agendas, the involvement of the food industry in these charities (through partnership arrangements) could be the genesis of opportunities for more meaningful engagement on factors driving food insecurity – to which they have the power to respond.

Beyond involvement in the provision itself, several large national NGOs and charities are mobilised by issues of food insecurity and rising reliance on food banks, as illustrated by their publications and press releases (for example, Cooper and Dumpleton, 2013; CPAG, 2013; Save the Children, 2013). Further potential opportunities reside in the political response of policy makers to the identifiable rise of emergency food provision. The All-Party Parliamentary Group on Hunger and Food Poverty in Britain could potentially provide opportunities for leveraging more substantive policy responses.

The question, then, becomes one of how to translate this movement and sense of injustice into something solution-based – while the food industry, policy makers, NGOs, VCS and public are engaged. To explore this question, this chapter utilises the right to food notion of 'policy frameworks', which open up and protect opportunities for all actors to exercise responsibility towards progressive realisation of the right to food.

The utility of the right to food

The right to food helps frame the practical conclusions that can be drawn from this research for two key reasons: first, it is well suited to current policy-making contexts, which incorporate multiple actors and interests; second, it helps us think about and understand the role of a diverse range of stakeholders.

The appropriateness of the right to food approach for the contemporary context lies in its affinity with both policy-making processes and the state's capacity to drive a comprehensive response in the UK today. Policy network analysis highlights the ways in which policy making is conducted not through formal institutions but rather through informal networks, which involve complex interplays between ministers, civil servants, pressure and interest groups and many others in the process of arriving at particular policies (Hudson et al., 2007; Richards and Smith, 2002). The right to food approach fits well within this networked reality and is particularly 'actionable' therein. It is inclusive of the wide variety of actors and groups that have a stake in the agenda, taking into account the complex roles played by each and every one of them. The right to food as a social ethic – a parent of policies in pursuit of this social good – may therefore be particularly helpful, insofar as it provides a loose framework that gives everyone the space to enact their responsibilities and to acknowledge the role of a wide variety of actors.

In addition to this affinity with the policy process, there is a rather realist factor with which the right to food approach may assist in progressively moving forward – namely, that in practice the state has (for reasons of necessity or ideology) little capacity (or political will) to comprehensively respond by itself to the problem of food insecurity. Politically and practically, we are facing a much leaner welfare state and an ever-increasing reluctance to interfere with any kind of market. This networked approach fits this reality, focusing as it does on other actors to take responsibilities alongside the state. The notion of the state as the duty bearer within this context, then, is particularly helpful. It places accountability with the state, but not responsibility for all actions towards progressive realisation of the right to food.

Roles and responsibilities of stakeholders

The right to food approach also holds utility through helping us to build a better picture of these different roles – to make space and account for the responsibilities of other actors, which need to be played out in these frameworks. General Comment 12 of the UN Economic and Social Council states that 'individuals, families, local communities, NGOs, civil society organisations, as well as the private business sector' all have responsibilities in the realisation of the right to food (CESCR, 1999). Employing this approach to thinking about solutions to food insecurity gives us an opportunity to ask and identify what these roles and responsibilities are in practice currently, what they should theoretically be in the future and which are yet to be explored.

In the context of the contemporary food system in the UK, individuals are often seen as consumers, with a corresponding role in shaping that system through purchasing power and exercising consumer choice (Kneafsey et al., 2013). However, the findings of this research problematise this traditional conceptualisation, instead highlighting the more complex and relational role some individuals play in terms of supporting friends and family (Ahluwalia et al., 1998; Hossain et al., 2011; Pfeiffer et al., 2011) or taking part in community-based emergency food provision.

The findings also question the role of communities. They suggest that local communities are increasingly assuming the responsibility for caring for local people in food insecurity – by setting up food banks or FareShare franchises, or engaging in local-level independent provision (independent food banks, soup runs and others). While there is much celebration of these endeavours, the findings also indicate a tension in the sense of 'duty' that drives these initiatives, as opposed to opportunism. There are a range of questions regarding the role and responsibilities of communities in realising the right to food in the UK, which remain unanswered. Questions sometimes raised by those inside emergency food movements include whether they are better placed to care for people in food insecurity – and whether they can care more effectively than the state.

In both practice and theory, there appears to be a particularly constructive role for NGOs to play in advocacy and campaigning for comprehensive responses to food insecurity and the realisation of the right to food. Several organisations are already involved in this kind of high-profile campaigning around food insecurity and the rise of food banks (Church Action on Poverty and Oxfam are particularly important examples). A key question, however, is how this work can be done constructively – without undermining the motivations of those involved in provision.

The role and responsibilities of government in relation to the right to food are clearly articulated: to respect, protect and fulfil the right to food. Previous research with consumers shows they too place considerable emphasis on government's role to realise food security. In Defra-funded research in 2010, 77% of survey respondents felt the government was 'responsible for ensuring basic food items are affordable for all UK residents', 64% felt it was the government's role to 'ensure UK residents have access to a wide choice of affordable nutritious food at all times' (Kneafsey et al., 2013, p.109) and workshop participants assigned overall responsibility for all aspects of food security to the government.

Many questions could be asked of the food industry's role and responsibilities in the realisation of the right to food. Importantly, the findings presented in the book have identified the ways in which the food industry works with the food charities under study. These relationships – based around providing access to surplus food within their supply chains, and the organisation of national food drives – raise key questions about the corporatisation of UK food charity. While there may be a productive role for the food industry within charitable food endeavours, its role beyond this is clearly critical (and likely where their key responsibilities actually lie). Kneafsey et al.'s (2013, p.109) research on consumer perceptions of responsibility for food security found that, 'in terms of affordability, "retailers" were assigned most responsibility after "government"'. However, consumers were sceptical about retailers' motivations, highlighting their accountability to shareholders; they therefore looked to government to 'temper market forces and ensure some degree of social responsibility' (Kneafsey et al., 2013, p.109).

The responsibility for private business would extend much wider – to include not only food producers and businesses involved in supply chains, but also (for example) financial institutions involved in futures trading, and many others. Importantly, it appears that the food industry's current role (beyond supporting charity) is not being engaged with in contemporary discussions of food insecurity. Much more work to establish the responsibilities of this sector in realising the human right to food is therefore required.

Final conclusions

Three sets of conclusions are drawn on the basis of the findings presented in this book, all framed by the right to food approach. The first is that there is a need to challenge minimalist approaches to understanding and responding to the problem of food insecurity. The second is that there is a need for rights-driven policies and frameworks, through which a range of stakeholders are held to account and facilitated to work towards the realisation of the right to food for all. The third is that emergency food provision could play a particularly important social and political role in the realisation of the right to food, providing individual care, advocacy and political pressure.

Conclusion 1: the need to challenge minimums

Like much poverty research – including the work of Lister (2004) and Townsend (1979) – this book has emphasised that food insecurity and food rights should not be understood in relation to minimums. Minimalist approaches that emphasise acute need (instead of wider vulnerabilities) and nutritionally minimal diets (instead of the important role food plays in social inclusion) are not progressive, and pose important challenges for the future realisation of the right to food. The first conclusion of the book is therefore the need to resist minimalist approaches – in relation to how need and food insecurity are defined, responses judged and solutions conceptualised.

This conclusion is drawn from findings showing that food adequacy is about much more than nutritional intake (Chapter Four) – it also relates to the social acceptability of the means by which food is acquired and the ways in which food experiences can be socially exclusive. Findings relating to the sustainability of food sources (Chapter Five) also highlight the importance of considering not only whether immediate need can be met now, but also whether it can continue to be met into the future. Findings relating to the effects of welfare retrenchment on the need for and shape of emergency food provision (Chapter Seven) also highlight that reductionist shifts in entitlements and increasingly conditioned social security provision have important impacts on people's ability to access adequate food. The findings of Chapter Six are particularly important for drawing this first conclusion, however, and provide evidence of how conceptualisations of crisis need for emergency food assistance are embedded within providers' appreciation of the wider vulnerabilities and underpinning drivers of experiences of food insecurity and poverty more generally. Furthermore, these initiatives' success is understood to relate to a range of relational and social contributions beyond the provision of a parcel of emergency food.

Broader conceptualisations and definitions of the problem of food insecurity emphasise the importance of not only dietary intake but also the experience of acquiring food and the sustainability of those acquisition sources into the future. They emphasise social acceptability and social inclusion, highlighting the important role food experiences have in shaping lived realities of exclusion and isolation. Similarly, the way in which need for emergency food provision is understood – often in terms of 'crisis' – should also be located within a wider understanding. Notions of crisis should be situated within a wider appreciation of the underpinning complexity and precarity of household experiences of food insecurity and poverty, and incorporate notions of mild and moderate levels of food insecurity.

Responses to experiences of food insecurity should also avoid minimalism. Instead of focusing on minimum nutrients, foods or incomes, responses should take into account social justice, inclusion and participation. While some responses are required that fulfil the human right to food, wider progressive responses are also required to focus on realising everyone's participation within socially accepted food experiences, and the enjoyment of food's facilitative social role.

Solutions to the problem of food insecurity should also be framed broadly; they should be ambitious and inclusive of all stakeholders. Conceptualisations of these solutions should strive not only to relieve – or even solve – food insecurity, but also for equitable and just food experiences that are secure into the future.

Conclusion 2: the importance of rights-based policies

The second key conclusion of the book is that more tangible steps need to be taken to facilitate the progressive realisation of the right to food in the UK. This conclusion is drawn from findings relating to the increasing prominence of and reliance on a system that is neither adequate nor sustainable by right to food standards (Chapters Four and Five). The fact that we have seen the growth of a system that can only respond to immediate need and that represents increasingly privatised and marginalised ways of caring for people in poverty (Chapter Six) at the same time as there has been a retrenchment of provision from the welfare state (Chapter Seven) means that, in order for food rights to be realised in the UK, clear frameworks for action are required.

In relation to emergency food provision, while the right to food approach sets out the roles and responsibilities for food charities such as emergency food providers, Special Rapporteur on the Right to Food, DeSchutter, was critical of circumstances in which the state comes to rely on charitable initiatives to protecting citizens against food insecurity. On returning from a visit to Canada in 2012, DeSchutter wrote: 'The reliance on food banks is symptomatic of a broken social protection system and the failure of the State to meet its obligations to its people' (DeSchutter, 2012b, p. 5). Within the context of many different actors, states as duty bearers are expected to 'take steps to achieve *progressively* the full realisation of the right to adequate food' (CESCR, 1999; emphasis in original). General Comment 12 also sets out that states should 'provide an environment that facilitates implementation' of the responsibilities of other actors. A clear, proactive role is therefore set out for governments, and – in so far as they are 'duty bearers' – accountability of ensuring progress towards this realisation lies with the state.

Two particular aspects will be important in realising the right to food in the UK and beyond: participation and democratisation (bringing those affected by hunger to the forefront of policy responses), and domestic legal and institutional infrastructure. National consultation and strategies will also be key. Bellows (2003) highlights the importance of reconceptualising the right to food through democratic participation (Bellows, 2003, p.264) and of 'centralising the needs and perspectives of those most vulnerable to household-based and food related violences' (p.273), including previously silenced voices. DeSchutter (2010) emphasises the participation of affected people in decision-making processes around the right to food – for example, through right to food strategies – as it 'ensures that real needs are identified and effectively responded to' (DeSchutter, 2010, p.7).

Legal frameworks are also essential for rights to be operationalised and claimed (Beuchelt and Vircow, 2012; DeSchutter, 2010). Indeed, DeSchutter (2010, p.1) describes the right to food as 'the right, for all, to have legal frameworks and strategies in place that further the realisation of the right to adequate food'. Specifically, McClain-Nhlapo (2004, p.3) argues that rights-based approaches 'allows claimants to assert and claim their rights, making the critical shift from treating hunger and food insecurity as a charitable endeavour to recognising adequate food as a right that must be protected by law'.

Constitutional law and other legal frameworks are key first steps in operationalising the right to food. Beuchelt and Vircow (2012, p.266) highlight that the right to food is enshrined in the constitutions of 40 countries, by the Food and Agriculture Organisation's estimates. Enshrining the right to food as a constitutional right is important, argues DeSchutter (2010, p.2), because it is the 'strongest possible basis the right to food can have, since all laws must conform to constitutional provisions'. In addition to constitutional law, framework law is required to provide legal provisions and obligations and stipulate governance objectives, as well as targets, goals, timeframes, accountability and monitoring (McClain-Nhlapo, 2004, p.2). The translation of the right to food into national law can, as DeSchutter (2010, p.5) observes, be undertaken in such a way as to formulate an 'overarching right to food framework' or 'include it in sectoral legislation' – such as fishers' rights. In order to ensure these laws have full effect and are fully realised, an institutional framework to support the right to food agenda must also be present to 'monitor and assess the right to food situation in a country' (DeSchutter, 2010, p.12).

For the right to food to be put into action after these structures have been put in place, national strategies are required to establish specific programmes and their implementation (DeSchutter, 2010; FAO, 2005). These strategies must 'be linked to pro-poor initiatives, must be credible and realistic and must identify concrete actions for the various duty bearers' (McClain-Nhlapo, 2004, p.3).

As a first step in the UK, a right to food consultation will be key. Such consultations can be an important way of articulating the right to food in particular country contexts, bringing together key stakeholders, sharing best practice and identifying current status and required actions on the right to food (McClain-Nhlapo, 2004, p.2).

DeSchutter (2010) outlines several key components necessary for improving the protection for the right to food:

1. Governments should adopt the right to food in their constitutions;
2. Framework laws should be established which incorporate participatory mechanisms;
3. Frameworks laws and national strategies should hold all actors (governmental and non-governmental) to account;
4. Institutions which are set up should be well resourced; and
5. Victims should have access to an independent judiciary or complaints mechanism.

Conclusion 3: the social and political role of emergency food provision in realising the right to food

As a mode of food provision and acquisition, emergency food provision poses a number of challenges from a right to food perspective. When condensing the findings of this research, a number of critiques can be levelled at this provision. The first is universality. Food charity is neither a population-wide response nor – critically – an entitlement. Furthermore, there are questions of accessibility regarding how access to food charity is managed, as well as the charity's accessibility and the thresholds it sets out when access is granted. The social injustice of food charity is also important from a right to food perspective; in terms of social acceptability (as discussed in Chapters Four and Five), food charity is outside of acceptable methods for acquiring food in the UK.

In relation to preventing food insecurity and enabling food access, in the first instance, charitable initiatives provide relief from the symptoms of food insecurity. While they may (when designed and managed appropriately) alleviate experiences of hunger, they are necessarily unable to solve the underlying drivers (see Lambie-Mumford et al., 2014). The food charities under study also emphasised responding to food insecurity crisis, rather than overcoming vulnerability to food insecurity. The right to food approach also requires emphasis on mild and moderate experiences and overcoming these – not just responding to acute need. Finally, there is the question of how far food charity may mask state accountability and responsibility. The ways in which this kind of charity may enable states to 'look the other way' (Riches, 2002, p.648) could be detrimental to ensuring that states act on their obligations to prevent and protect against food insecurity as a prerequisite for the realisation of the human right to food.

The food acquisition and provision role of emergency food provision is therefore limited as part of the progressive realisation of the right to food. Having said this, based on the research presented here, these initiatives may have particularly important social and political roles to play.

Emergency food provision may have a constructive role to play at the individual and local levels. The findings of Chapters Four and Six in particular highlight that emergency food projects play a more complex role than is first apparent. While food insecurity outcomes from the food on offer and the mechanisms for obtaining it may be limited, emergency food providers play a social role as spaces of care and facilitators of social support and welfare networks. At an individual level, the research indicates that these initiatives can provide important spaces of care – but there can also be social outcomes at the community level. Through providing opportunities for volunteering and community participation, these organisations facilitate social capital; they could also strengthen social support networks by connecting community provision and signposting. This fits with the right to food approach, which is driven not only by the impetus to solve the problem of food insecurity but also by the recognition that more is required, that more issues and actors need to be involved and that there are wider drivers of poverty at work.

The findings of Chapters Six and Seven highlight the important political role these organisations have and the ways they speak to politics and policy – individually, collectively and alongside stakeholder faith groups, individual donors and other interested NGOs. Through conversations with policy makers, campaigning, advocacy and engagement with the work of high-profile NGOs, emergency food providers can play a proactive role in shaping the politics of food insecurity.

Based on the findings of this book, it therefore appears that, while emergency food providers set out to alleviate food insecurity, their principal contributions to the realisation of the right to food may be social and political. As emergency food provision is not able to provide adequate protection from food insecurity when it occurs by a right to food standard, perhaps it has a role to play in facilitating and enabling the right to food, given the sociopolitical contributions organisations can make. Potentially, then, the most constructive contribution of emergency food charities to realising the right to food may be an enabling one – holding states accountable to their responsibility to respect, protect and fulfil the right to food through advocacy work and national campaigning, and actively facilitating access to food for individuals in local communities by connecting social support networks, welfare safety nets and signposting to other services.

Recommendations

Some recommendations are offered here to end the book, based on the research findings and conclusions. Recommendations are suggested for a range of stakeholders, including emergency food providers, policy makers, NGOs, the food industry, local communities and individuals and researchers.

Emergency food charities

Emergency food charities should emphasise their social and political contribution to progressive responses to food insecurity and realising the human right to food in the UK. In relation to Conclusion 3, they could also have a role to play in realising the right to food through forming a 'social movement', drawing attention to the issue of food insecurity and calling for a rights-based solution. A social movement is 'a network of associations, groups and individuals that are allied with each other through sharing a particular programme of action or sense of identity' (Scott, 2001, p.112). Given the profile of the issue of hunger and endeavour of emergency food provision, such a movement could have a potentially powerful voice in the current context, and could help to drive a right to food agenda – drawing on advocacy and campaigning work at national and local levels.

Whether or not they form part of a wider sociopolitical movement, the work of individual organisations in this area could also be important. Providers could have a specifically political role to play in the realisation of the right to food through advocacy and campaigning work, and specifically maximising the amount of work they do speaking to wider political processes and trying to shift structural determinants of food insecurity (for example, low income or problems with the social security system). This is a role that The Trussell Trust in particular works to fulfil at the moment (as highlighted at various points in this book); and this conclusion advocates for this role to continue and expand.

Specifically, emergency food providers should focus on:

- Their signposting work and connecting poverty services locally;
- Their advocacy and campaigning work at local, devolved and national levels; and
- Being aware of the symbiotic relationship between emergency food provision and the welfare state, and doing all they can to not become a permanent substitute for the (welfare) state.

Policy makers

Nationally, policy makers should focus on the rising use of emergency food provision and the problem of food insecurity. Right to food strategies should be adopted for guiding tangible policy responses that also draw on other actors and hold them to account. Given the lack of data and understanding of the problem of food insecurity and given how problematic these systems are as standalone responses, first steps towards this should be:

- Establishing and funding a regular systematic measure of food insecurity in the UK; and
- Beginning a consultation on the right to food and developing a comprehensive timetable for action, bringing in all Whitehall departments and the full range of stakeholders across civil society, government and the private sector.

NGOs

NGOs should engage more with rights-based discourses to guide campaigning and advocacy. This could be particularly constructive, given that the state has yet to enact its role as duty bearer and communities and emergency food providers are busy responding to need. A key challenge here is that human rights are not very fashionable in UK policy making and governance; some prominent NGOs will use this discourse with international work, but not so much in their UK work. Nonetheless, NGOs should also maintain a focus on holding government to account over the rise of food insecurity and increasing reliance on emergency food provision. Particular recommendations for NGOs are:

- To lobby for a UK right to food strategy;
- To support emergency food providers by giving voice to the evidence they collect around levels and drivers of need; and
- To hold the food industry to account, as well as the government.

The food industry

The food industry should engage with the issue of food insecurity beyond supporting food charity as part of corporate social responsibility. Emergency food provision can be seen as a symptom of an unsustainable food system, so the question of what the food industry could and should do is urgent. The industry – specifically retailers – should look at fairness across their food chains, and specifically:

- How the structure of their retailing (planning and location of stores), pricing and offers structures impact on food insecurity in the UK; and
- Their role as employers in determining employees' experiences of food insecurity in relation to zero-hour contracts and living wages.

Local communities and individuals

In addition to their engagement in helping others in their social networks or getting involved in an emergency food project, local communities and individuals should join wider discussions at local authority, devolved and national policy levels around food insecurity and the right to food.

Researchers

Finally, when exploring the vast range of potential questions for studying this phenomenon, researchers should engage more fully with the right to food framework and ask questions about constructive ways forward.

References

Ahluwalia, I.B., Dodds, J.M. and Baligh, M., 1998, Social support and coping behaviors of low-income families experiencing food insufficiency in North Carolina, *Health Education & Behavior*, 25, 5, 599–612.

Alcock, P., 2010, Partnership and mainstreaming: voluntary action under new labour, *Third Sector Research Centre Working Paper*, 32, www.birmingham.ac.uk/generic/tsrc/documents/tsrc/working-papers/working-paper-32.pdf.

Anderson, M., 2013, Beyond food security to realizing food rights in the US, *Journal of Rural Studies*, 29, 113–22.

Anderson, S.A., 1990, Core indicators of nutritional state for difficult-to-sample populations, *The Journal of Nutrition*, 120, 11, 1555–1600.

Backman, G., Hunt, P., Khosla, R., Jaramillo-Strouss, C., Fikre, B.M., Rumble, C., Pevalin, D., Páez, D.A., Pineda, M.A., Frisancho, A., Tarco, D., Motlagh, M., Farcasanu, D. and Vladescu, C., 2008, Health systems and a right to health: an assessment of 194 countries, *The Lancet*, 372, 9655, 2047–85.

BBC, 2014, Councils spending £3m on food poverty and food banks, *BBC News*, 3 March, www.bbc.co.uk/news/uk-26369558.

Beattie, J., 2014, 27 Bishops slam David Cameron's welfare reforms as creating a national crisis in unprecedented attack, *Daily Mirror*, 19 February, www.mirror.co.uk/news/uk-news/27-bishops-slam-david-camerons-3164033.

Beatty, C. and Fothergill, S., 2013, *Hitting the poorest places hardest: the local and regional impact of welfare reform*, Sheffield: Centre for Regional Economic and Social Research, Sheffield Hallam University, www4.shu.ac.uk/research/cresr/sites/shu.ac.uk/files/hitting-poorest-places-hardest_0.pdf.

Bellows, A., 2003, Exposing violences: using women's human rights theory to reconceptualise food rights, *Journal of Agricultural and Environmental Ethics*, 16, 249–79.

Berner, M. and O'Brien, K., 2004, The shifting pattern of food security support: food stamp and food bank usage in North Carolina, *Nonprofit and Voluntary Sector Quarterly*, 33, 4, 655–72.

Beuchelt, T.D. and Vircow, D., 2012, Food sovereignty or the human right to food? Which concept serves better as international development policy for global hunger?, *Agriculture and Human Values*, 29, 259–73.

Beveridge, W., 1942, *Extracts from the Beveridge Report, detailing key aims and vision*, National Archives, www.nationalarchives.gov.uk/education/resources/attlees-britain/beveridge-report/.

Bhattarai, G.R., Duffy, P.A. and Raymond, J., 2005, Use of food pantries and food stamps in low-income households in the United States, *Journal of Consumer Affairs*, 39, 2, 276–98.

Bible Societies, The, 1994, *Good news bible*, London: Harper Collins.

Bickel, G., Nord, M., Price, C., Hamilton, W. and Cook, H., 2000, *Guide to measuring household food security*, US Department of Agriculture Food and Nutrition Service, www.fns.usda.gov/guide-measuring-household-food-security-revised-2000.

Blackburn, D., 2013, George Osborne's benefits speech: full text, *The Spectator*, 2 April, http://blogs.spectator.co.uk/2013/04/george-osbornes-benefits-speech-full-text/.

Boyle, D., 2014, Almost ONE million Britons visit food banks following 162 percent jump in the number of people seeking emergency help, *The Daily Mail*, 16 January, www.dailymail.co.uk/news/article-2605661/Almost-ONE-million-Britons-seek-food-bank-help-following-162-percent-jump-number-people-seeking-emergency-food-help.html.

Butler, P., 2012, Breadline Britain: councils fund food banks to plug holes in welfare state, *The Guardian*, 21 August, www.theguardian.com/society/2012/aug/21/councils-invest-food-banks-welfare-cuts.

Butler, P., 2013, Welfare cuts: a tale of two food bank vouchers, *The Guardian*, 6 September, www.theguardian.com/society/patrick-butler-cuts-blog/2013/sep/06/welfare-cuts-trussell-trust-tale-of-two-food-banks-jobcentres.

Butler, P., 2014a, Scottish government report links welfare reform to food bank growth, *The Guardian*, 16 January, www.theguardian.com/society/patrick-butler-cuts-blog/2014/jan/16/scottish-govt-links-welfare-cuts-to-rise-in-food-banks.

Butler, P., 2014b, DWP and food bank referrals: 'a way to keep your job but salve your conscience', *The Guardian*, 17 March, www.theguardian.com/society/patrick-butler-cuts-blog/2014/mar/17/food-bank-referrals-jobcentre-welfare.

Cabinet Office, 2010, *Building the big society*, www.gov.uk/government/publications/building-the-big-society.

Caraher, M., Dixon, P., Lang, T. and Carr-Hill, R., 1998, Access to healthy foods, part I: barriers to accessing healthy foods: differentials by gender, social class, income and mode of transport, *Health Education Journal*, 57, 3, 191–201.

CEBR (Centre for Economics and Business Research), 2013, *Hard to swallow: the facts about food poverty*, CEBR, file:///C:/Users/jm16502/Chrome%20Local%20Downloads/Facts+about+Food+Poverty+Re portFINAL.pdf.

CESCR (Committee on Economic, Social and Cultural Rights), 1999, *Substantive issues arising in the implementation of the international covenant on economic, social and cultural rights: General comment 12 (twentieth session, 1999, the right to adequate food (Art. 11)*, Geneva: United Nations, www.fao.org/fileadmin/templates/righttofood/documents/RTF_publications/EN/General_Comment_12_EN.pdf.

Channel 4 News, 2014, The truth about food banks: dependency or welfare crisis?, 20 February, www.channel4.com/news/food-banks-key-questions-hunger-austerity-welfare-cuts.

Chilton, M. and Rose, D., 2009, A rights-based approach to food insecurity in the United States, *American Journal of Public Health*, 99, 7, 1203–11.

Chorley, M., 2013, Don't call people on benefits 'scroungers', Archbishop of Canterbury warns ministers, *The Daily Mail*, 9 July, www.dailymail.co.uk/news/article-2358741/Dont-people-benefits-scroungers-Archbishop-Canterbury-warns-ministers.html.

Church Urban Fund, 2013, Guide to welfare reforms 2010–2017, www.cuf.org.uk/guide-to-welfare-reforms-2010-2017.

Clarke, A., Hill, L., Marshall, B., Monk, S., Pereira, I., Thompson, E., Whitehead, C. and Williams, P., 2014, Evaluation of removal of the Spare Room Subsidy: Interim report, Research Report 882, Department for Work and Pensions and Government Social Research, https://www.gov.uk/government/uploads/system/uploads/attachment_data/file/329948/rr882-evaluation-of-removal-of-the-spare-room-subsidy.pdf.

Cloke, P., May, J. and Johnsen, S., 2010, *Swept up lives? Re-envisioning the homeless city*, London: Wiley Blackwell.

Coleman-Jensen, A., 2011, Working for peanuts: non-standard work and food insecurity across household structure, *Journal of Family and Economic Issues*, 32, 1, 84–97.

Coleman-Jensen, A., Gregory, C. and Singh, A., 2014a, *Household food security in the United States in 2013*, Washington, DC: US Department of Agriculture, Economic Research Service, www.ers.usda.gov/webdocs/publications/err173/48787_err173.pdf.

Coleman-Jensen, A., Gregory, C. and Singh, A., 2014b, *Household food security in the United States in 2013: Statistical supplement*, Washington, DC: Department of Agriculture, Economic Research Service, www.ers.usda.gov/publications/pub-details/?pubid=42801.

Conservative Home, 2012, *Food banks ARE part of the Big Society – but the problem they are tackling is not new*, www.conservativehome.com/localgovernment/2012/12/council-should-encourage-food-banks.html.

Cooper, N. and Dumpleton, S., 2013, *Walking the breadline: The scandal of food poverty in 21st century Britain*, Oxfam & Church Action on Poverty, http://policy-practice.oxfam.org.uk/publications/walking-the-breadline-the-scandal-of-food-poverty-in-21st-century-britain-292978.

Costello, H.E., 2007, Hunger in our own backyard: the face of hunger in the United States, *Nutrition in Clinical Practice*, 22, 587–90.

CPAG (Child Poverty Action Group), 2013, *'Foodbanks first' jobseekers cut and welfare cap will rack up economic costs of child poverty*, 26 June, www.cpag.org.uk/content/foodbanks-first-jobseekers-cut-and-welfare-cap-will-rack-economic-costs-child-poverty.

Crawley, H., Hemmings, J. and Price, N., 2011, *Coping with destitution: Survival and livelihood strategies of refused asylum seekers living in the UK*, Oxfam, http://policy-practice.oxfam.org.uk/publications/coping-with-destitution-survival-and-livelihood-strategies-of-refused-asylum-se-121667.

Daily Record, 2014, Growing demand for foodbanks is 'inextricably linked' to welfare reforms, charities tell MSPs, *Daily Record*, 4 March, www.dailyrecord.co.uk/news/politics/growing-demand-foodbanks-inextricably-linked-3206310.

Daponte, B., Osborne, A., Haviland and Kadane, J.B., K., 2004, To what degree does food assistance help poor households acquire enough food? A joint examination of public and private sources of food assistance, *Journal of Poverty*, 2, 8, 63–87.

Daponte, B.O. and Bade, S., 2006, How the private food assistance network evolved: interactions between public and private responses to hunger, *Nonprofit and Voluntary Sector Quarterly*, 35, 4, 668–90.

Davis, A., Hirsch, D. and Padley, M., 2014, *A minimum income standard for the UK in 2014*, York: Joseph Rowntree Foundation, www.jrf.org.uk/report/minimum-income-standard-uk-2014.

Davis, A., Hirsch, D., Smith, N., Beckhelling, J. and Padley, M., 2012, *A minimum income standard for the UK in 2012*: *Keeping up in hard times*, York: Joseph Rowntree Foundation, www.jrf.org.uk/sites/default/files/jrf/migrated/files/minimum-income-standards-2012-full.pdf.

De Marco, M. and Thorburn, S., 2009, The relationship between income and food insecurity among Oregon residents: does social support matter?, *Public Health Nutrition*, 12, 11, 2104–12.

Dean, H., 2008, Social policy and human rights: re-thinking the engagement, *Social Policy and Society*, 7, 1, 1–12.

Dean, H., 2009, Critiquing capabilities: the distractions of a beguiling concept, *Critical Social Policy*, 29, 2, 261–73.

Defra (Department for Environment, Food and Rural Affairs), 2006, *Food security and the UK: An evidence and analysis paper*, London: Defra, http://archive.defra.gov.uk/evidence/economics/foodfarm/reports/documents/foodsecurity.pdf. Accessed 10 February 2017.

Defra, 2014, Food statistics pocket book: In year update, London: Defra, www.gov.uk/government/uploads/system/uploads/attachment_data/file/315418/foodpocketbook-2013update-29may14.pdf.

DeSchutter, O., 2010, *Countries tackling hunger with a right to food approach: Briefing note 01, May 2010*, www2.ohchr.org/english/issues/food/docs/Briefing_Note_01_May_2010_EN.pdf.

DeSchutter, O., 2012a, *HLPE report on social protection for food security and CFS decision box on social protection for food security*, Office of the High Commissioner for Human Rights (OHCHR), www.ohchr.org/Documents/Issues/Food/20120703_SRFoodCommentsSocialProtection.pdf.

DeSchutter, O., 2012b, *Visit to Canada from 6 to 16 May 2012, end of mission statement*, 16 May, Ottowa: United Nations.

DeSchutter, O., 2013, *Interim report of the Special Rapporteur on the right to food*, United Nations, https://documents-dds-ny.un.org/doc/UNDOC/GEN/N13/421/78/PDF/N1342178.pdf?OpenElement.

DeSchutter, O. and Sepulveda, M., 2012, *Underwriting the poor: A global fund for social protection, Briefing note 07: October 2012*, OHCHR, www.ohchr.org/Documents/Issues/Food/20121009_GFSP_en.pdf.

Dimbleby, H. and Vincent, J., 2013, *The school food plan*, London: Department for Education, www.gov.uk/government/publications/the-school-food-plan.

Dowler, E., 1997, Budgeting for food on a low income in the UK: the case of lone-parent families, *Food Policy*, 22, 5, 405–17.

Dowler, E., 2003, Food and poverty in Britain: rights and responsibilities, in E. Dowler and C. Jones Finer (eds) *The welfare of food: Rights and responsibilities in a changing world*, Oxford: Blackwell, 140–59.

Dowler, E. and Lambie-Mumford, H., 2014, *Food aid: Living with food insecurity*, Working Papers of the Communities & Culture Network, www.communitiesandculture.org/files/2013/01/Living-with-Food-Insecurity-CCN-Report.pdf.

Dowler, E. and Lambie-Mumford, H., 2015, How can households eat in austerity? Challenges for social policy in the UK, *Social Policy and Society*, 14, 3, 417–28.

Dowler, E. and O'Connor, D., 2012, Rights-based approaches to addressing food poverty and food insecurity in Ireland and UK, *Social Science and Medicine*, 74, 44–51.

Dowler, E., Kneafsey, M., Lambie, H., Inman, A. and Collier, R., 2011, Thinking about 'food security': engaging with UK consumers, *Critical Public Health*, 21, 4, 403–16.

Dowler, E., Turner, S.A. and Dobson, B., 2001, *Poverty bites: Food, health and poor families*, London: CPAG.

Dugan, E., 2014, The real cost-of-living crisis: five million British children 'sentenced to life of poverty thanks to welfare reforms', *The Independent*, 27 May, www.independent.co.uk/news/uk/politics/the-real-cost-of-living-crisis-five-million-british-children-face-life-of-poverty-thanks-to-welfare-9442061.html.

DWP (Department for Work and Pensions), 2012, *Housing benefit: Size criteria for people renting in the social rented sector, equality impact assessment*, London: DWP, www.gov.uk/government/uploads/system/uploads/attachment_data/file/220154/eia-social-sector-housing-under-occupation-wr2011.pdf.

DWP, 2013, *Jobseeker's Allowance: Overview of revised sanctions regime*, London: DWP, https://www.gov.uk/government/uploads/system/uploads/attachment_data/file/238839/jsa-overview-of-revised-sanctions-regime.pdf

DWP, 2014a, Jobseeker's Allowance and Employment and Support Allowance sanctions, London: DWP, www.gov.uk/government/collections/jobseekers-allowance-sanctions.

DWP, 2014b, Benefit Cap: Analysis of outcomes of capped claimants, London: DWP, https://www.gov.uk/government/uploads/system/uploads/attachment_data/file/385970/benefit-cap-analysis-of-_outcomes-of-capped-claimants.pdf

Elder-Vass, D., 2010, *The causal power of social structures: Emergency, structure and agency*, Cambridge: Cambridge University Press.

Ellison, M. and Fenger, M., 2013, Social investment, protection and inequality in the new economy and politics of welfare in Europe, *Social Policy and Society*, 12, 4, 611–24.

End Hunger Fast, n.d., *End Hunger Fast*, http://endhungerfast.co.uk/.

End Hunger UK, n.d., *End Hunger UK*, http://endhungeruk.org/.

Engler-Stringer, R. and Berenbaum, S., 2007, Exploring food security with collective kitchens participants in three Canadian cities, *Qualitative Health Research*, 17, 1, 75–84.

FAO (Food and Agriculture Organization), 1983, *World food security: A reappraisal of the concepts and approaches* (Director-General's report), Rome: United Nations.

FAO, 2005, *Voluntary guidelines to support the progressive realisations of the right to adequate food in the context of national security*, Rome: United Nations, www.fao.org/docrep/009/y7937e/y7937e00.htm.

FAO, 2006, *Food security policy brief*, ftp://ftp.fao.org/es/ESA/policybriefs/pb_02.pdf.

FAO, 2016, *Methods for estimating comparable prevalence rates of food insecurity experienced by adults throughout the world: Technical report*, www.fao.org/3/a-i4830e.pdf.

FareShare, 2014, *Our history*, www.fareshare.org.uk/our-history/.

FareShare, n.d.a, *About us*, www.fareshare.org.uk/about-us/.

FareShare, n.d.b, *FareShare*, www.fareshare.org.uk/.

Farnsworth, K., 2011, From economic crisis to a new age of austerity: the UK, in K. Farnsworth and Z. Irving (eds) *Social policy and challenging times: Economic crisis and welfare systems*, Bristol: Policy Press, 251-270.

Farnsworth, K. and Irving, Z., 2011, Responding to the challenges: some concluding remarks on welfare futures in changed circumstances, in K. Farnsworth and Z. Irving (eds) *Social policy and challenging times: Economic crisis and welfare systems*, Bristol: Policy Press, 271-278.

FEBA (European Federation of Food Banks), n.d., *European Federation of Food Banks*, www.eurofoodbank.eu/.

Feichtinger, E., 1997, Looking beyond nutrients: towards a more holistic view of poverty and food, in B. M. Köhler, E. Feichtinger, E. Barlösius and E. Dowler (eds) *Poverty and food in welfare societies*, Berlin: Sigma Ed, 47-57.

Food Poverty Inquiry, 2014a, *Terms of reference*, http://foodpovertyinquiry.org/terms-of-reference/.

Food Poverty Inquiry, 2014b, *Feeding Britain: A strategy for zero hunger in England, Wales, Scotland and Northern Ireland: The report of the All-Party Parliamentary Inquiry*, https://foodpovertyinquiry.files.wordpress.com/2014/12/food-poverty-feeding-britain-final.pdf.

Food Poverty Inquiry, 2014c, *An evidence review for the All-Party Parliamentary Inquiry into Hunger in the United Kingdom*, https://foodpovertyinquiry.files.wordpress.com/2014/12/food-poverty-appg-evidence-review-final.pdf.

Garthwaite, K., 2016 *Hunger pains: Life inside foodbank Britain*, Bristol: Policy Press.

Garthwaite, K. A., Collins, P. J. and Bambra, C., 2015, Food for thought: an ethnographic study of negotiating ill health and food insecurity in a UK foodbank, *Social Science and Medicine*, 132, 38–44.

Goode, J., 2012, Feeding the family when then the wolf's at the door: the impact of over-indebtedness on contemporary foodways in low-income families in the UK, *Food and Foodways: Explorations in the History and Culture of Human Nourishment*, 20, 1, 8–30.

Goodman, D., DuPuis, E.M. and Goodman, M.K., 2011, *Alternative food networks: Knowledge, practice, and politics*, Abingdon: Routledge.

Gordon, D., Levitas, R., Pantazis, C., Patsios, D., Payne, S., Townsend, P., Adelman, L., Ashworth, K., Middleton, S., Bradshaw, J. and Williams, J., 2000, *Poverty and social exclusion in Britain*, York: Joseph Rowntree Foundation.

Gordon, D. and Pantazis, C., 1997, Measuring poverty, in D. Gordon and C. Pantazis (eds) *Breadline Britain in the 1990s*, Aldershot: Ashgate.

Green, M. and Lawson, V., 2011, Recentring care: interrogating the commodification of care, *Social & Cultural Geography*, 12, 6, 639–54.

Gregory, L., 2014, Food banks show welfare is not working, *Progress Online*, 31 March, www.progressonline.org.uk/2014/03/31/79489/.

Hansard, 2013, *Food banks*, House of Commons debate, 18 December, column 806, www.publications.parliament.uk/pa/cm201314/cmhansrd/cm131218/debtext/131218-0003.htm.

Hansard, 2016, Household food insecurity, House of Commons debate, 6 December, vol. 618, https://hansard.parliament.uk/Commons/2016-12-06/debates/8EBAC4F7-9890-49CE-A2C1-7E75CECE1731/HouseholdFoodInsecurity#contribution-F09BF2B0-9AE6-4D6A-B9EF-3ADCD41BB459.

Hanson, M., 2013, Food banks: just the start of the government's 'big society' plan, *The Guardian*, 10 June, www.theguardian.com/society/2013/jun/10/food-banks-government-big-society.

Hay, C., 2005, Too important to leave to the economists? The political economy of welfare retrenchment, *Social Policy and Society*, 4, 2, 197–205.

Health Canada, n.d., *Household food insecurity in Canada: Overview*, www.hc-sc.gc.ca/fn-an/surveill/nutrition/commun/insecurit/index-eng.php.

Hendricks, S.L. and McIntyre, A., 2014, Between markets and masses: food assistance and food banks in South Africa, in G. Riches and T. Silvasti (eds) *First world hunger revisited: Food charity or the right to food?* Basingstoke: Palgrave Macmillan, 117–30.

Hick, R., 2012, The capability approach: insights for a new poverty focus, *Journal of Social Policy*, 41, 2, 291–308.

Hirsch, D., 2013, *A minimum income standard for the UK in 2013*, York: Joseph Rowntree Foundation, www.jrf.org.uk/report/minimum-income-standard-uk-2013.

Hirsch, D., 2015a, *A minimum income standard for the UK in 2015: Summary*, York: Joseph Rowntree Foundation, www.jrf.org.uk/report/minimum-income-standard-uk-2013.

Hirsch, D., 2015b, *A minimum income standard for the UK in 2015*, Joseph Rowntree Foundation, www.jrf.org.uk/sites/default/files/jrf/migrated/files/MIS-2015-full.pdf.

Hitchman, C., Christie, I., Harrison, M. and Lang, T., 2002, *Inconvenience food: The struggle to eat well on a low income*, London: Demos.

Hosie, A. and Lamb, M., 2013, Human rights and social policy: challenges and opportunities for social research and its use as evidence in the protection and promotion of human rights in Scotland, *Social Policy and Society*, 12, 2, 191–203.

Hossain, N., Byrne, B., Campbell, A., Harrison, E., McKinley, B. and Shah, P., 2011, *The impact of the global economic downturn on communities and poverty in the UK*, York: Joseph Rowntree Foundation, www.jrf.org.uk/sites/default/files/jrf/migrated/files/experiences-of-economic-downturn-full.pdf.

Hudson, J., Lowe, S., Oscroft, N. and Snell, C., 2007, Activating policy networks: a case study of local environmental policy-making in the United Kingdom, *Policy Studies*, 28, 1, 55–70.

Isiah 58:6–7, *Good news bible*, London: Harper Collins.

Jackson, P. and Connanx Group, C., 2013, *Food words*, London: Bloomsbury.

Jarosz, L., 2011, Defining world hunger: scale and neoliberal ideology in international food security policy discourse, *Food, Culture and Society*, 14, 1, 117–36.

Joint Committee on Human Rights, 2004, *The International Covenant on Economic, Social and Cultural Rights*, London: Houses of Parliament, www.publications.parliament.uk/pa/jt200304/jtselect/jtrights/183/183.pdf.

Jowitt, J., 2014, Strivers v shirkers: the language of the welfare debate, *The Guardian*, 8 January, www.theguardian.com/politics/2013/jan/08/strivers-shirkers-language-welfare.

Just Fair, 2014, *Going hungry? The human right to food in the UK*, www.just-fair.co.uk/about1-c21gp.

Kirkpatrick, S.I. and Tarasuk, V., 2011, Housing circumstances are associated with household food access among low-income urban families, *Journal of Urban Health*, 88, 2, 284–96.

Kirkup, J., 2013, Autumn statement 2013: Britain can no longer afford welfare state, warns Osborne, *The Telegraph*, 2 December, www.telegraph.co.uk/finance/budget/10487295/Autumn-Statement-2013-Britain-can-no-longer-afford-welfare-state-warns-Osborne.html.

Kneafsey, M., Cox, R., Holloway, L., Dowler, E., Venn, L. and Tuomainen, H., 2008, *Reconnecting consumers, producers and food: Exploring alternatives*, Oxford: Berg.

Kneafsey, M., Dowler, E., Lambie-Mumford, H., Inman, I. and Collier, R., 2013, Consumers and food security: uncertain or empowered?, *Journal of Rural Studies*, 29, 101–12.

Kõre, J., 2014, Hunger and food aid in Estonia: a local authority and family obligation, in G. Riches and T. Silvasti (eds) *First world hunger revisited: Food charity or the right to food?*, Basingstoke: Palgrave Macmillan, 57-71.

Lambie, H., 2011, *The Trussell Trust Foodbank Network: Exploring the growth of foodbanks across the UK*, Coventry: Coventry University.

Lambie-Mumford, H., 2013, 'Every Town should have one': emergency food banking in the UK, *Journal of Social Policy*, 42, 1, 73–89.

Lambie-Mumford, H., 2014, *Food bank provision & welfare reform in the UK: SPERI British political economy brief no. 4*, http://speri.dept.shef.ac.uk/wp-content/uploads/2014/01/SPERI-British-Political-Economy-Brief-No4-Food-bank-provision-welfare-reform-in-the-UK.pdf.

Lambie-Mumford, H., 2015, Britain's hunger crisis: where's the social policy?, in Z. Irving, M. Fenger and J. Hudson (eds) *Social Policy Review 27*, Bristol: Policy Press, 13–31.

Lambie-Mumford, H. and Dowler, E., 2014, Rising use of 'food aid' in the United Kingdom, *British Food Journal*, 116, 9, 1418–25.

Lambie-Mumford, H. and Dowler, E., 2015, Hunger, food charity and social policy: challenges faced by the emerging evidence base, *Social Policy and Society*, 14, 3, 497–506.

Lambie-Mumford, H., Crossley, D., Jensen, E., Verbeke, M. and Dowler, E., 2014, *Household food security: A review of food aid*, London: Defra, www.gov.uk/government/publications/food-aid-research-report.

Lancet, The, 2008, The right to health: from rhetoric to reality, *The Lancet*, 372, 9655, 2001.

Lang, T., Barling, D. and Caraher, M., 2010, *Food policy: Integrating health, environment and society*, Oxford: Oxford University Press.

Lawson, V., 2007, Geographies of care and responsibility, *Annals of the Association of American Geographers*, 97, 1, 1–11.

Lister, R., 2004, *Poverty*, Cambridge: Polity.

Local Government Association, 2014, *Government should rethink scrapping of £347 million emergency welfare fund, councils urge*, media release, 24 February.

Local Government Association, 2015, LGA response to the Local Government Finance Settlement, media release, 4 February, http://www.local.gov.uk/web/guest/media-releases/-/journal_content/56/10180/6967973/NEWS.

Long, R., 2015, *School meals and nutritional standards: Standard note SN/SP/4195*, London: House of Commons, http://researchbriefings.parliament.uk/ResearchBriefing/Summary/SN04195.

Loopstra, R. and Tarasuk, V., 2012, The relationship between food banks and household food insecurity among low-income Toronto families, *Canadian Public Policy*, 38, 4, 497–514.

Loopstra, R. and Tarasuk, V., 2013, What does increasing severity of food insecurity indicate for food insecure families? Relationships between severity of food insecurity and indicators of material hardship and constrained food purchasing, *Journal of Hunger and Environmental Nutrition*, 8, 337–49.

Loopstra, R., Fladderjohann, J., Reeves, A., and Stuckler, D., 2016, The impact of benefit sanctioning on food insecurity: a dynamic cross-area study of food bank usage in the UK, *University of Oxford sociology working papers: Paper no. 20016-03*, www.sociology.ox.ac.uk/working-papers/the-impact-of-benefit-sanctioning-on-food-insecurity-a-dynamic-cross-area-study-of-food-bank-usage-in-the-uk.html.

Loopstra, R., Reeves, A., Taylor-Robinson, D., McKee, M. and Stuckler, D., 2015, Austerity, sanctions, and the rise of food banks in the UK, *British Medical Journal*, 350, 1775.

Lucas, P., Jessiman, T. and Cameron, A., 2015, Healthy Start: The use of welfare food vouchers by low-income parents in England, *Social Policy and Society*, 14, 3, 457–70.

Mabli, J., Cohen, R., Potter, F. and Zhao, Z., 2010, *Hunger in America 2010: National report prepared for Feeding America*, New Jersey: Mathematica Policy Research Inc., www.mathematica-mpr.com/our-publications-and-findings/publications/hunger-in-america-2010-national-report-prepared-for-feeding-america.

Mack, J., 1985, How poor is too poor? Defining poverty, in J. Mack and S. Lansley (eds) *Poor Britain*, London: George Allen & Unwin.

MacMillan, T. and Dowler, E., 2011, Just and sustainable? Examining the rhetoric and potential realities of UK food security, *Journal of Agricultural and Environmental Ethics*, 25, 2, 181–204.

Marshall, T.H., 1950, *Citizenship and social class*, London: Pluto.

Matthew 25:35–40, *Good news bible*, London: Harper Collins.

Maxwell, S., 1996, Food security: a post-modern perspective, *Food Policy*, 21, 2, 155–70.

McClain-Nhlapo, C., 2004, *Implementing a human rights approach to food security*, Washington DC: International Food Policy Research Institute, http://ebrary.ifpri.org/utils/getfile/collection/p15738coll2/id/64619/filename/64620.pdf.

McGlone, P., Dobson, B., Dowler, E. and Nelson, M., 1999, *Food projects and how they work*, York: Joseph Rowntree Foundation, www.jrf.org.uk/report/food-projects-and-how-they-work.

Meah, A., 2013, Shopping, in P. Jackson (ed.) *Food Words*, London: Bloomsbury, 197–200.

Mechlem, K., 2004, Food security and the right to food in the discourse of the United Nations, *European Law Journal*, 10, 5, 631–48.

Midgley, J.L., 2014, The logics of surplus food redistribution, *Journal of Environmental Planning and Management*, 57, 12, 1872–92.

Moore, S., 2012, 2012 has been the year of the food bank, *The Guardian*, 19 December, www.theguardian.com/commentisfree/2012/dec/19/2012-year-of-the-food-bank.

Morris, N., 2013, Hungrier than ever: Britain's use of food banks triples, *The Independent*, 15 October, www.independent.co.uk/news/uk/home-news/hungrier-than-ever-britain-s-use-of-food-banks-triples-8882340.html.

Mould, C., 2014, The £100,000 raised by readers for *Mirror's* Christmas Appeal will make a massive difference to hungry families, *The Mirror*, 4 January, www.mirror.co.uk/news/uk-news/100000-raised-readers-mirrors-christmas-2985176.

NHS, 2015, *The School Fruit and Vegetable Scheme (SFVS)*, www.nhs.uk/Livewell/5ADAY/Pages/Schoolscheme.aspx.

Nielsen, A., Bøker Lund, T. and Holm, L., 2015, The taste of 'the end of the month', and how to avoid it: coping with restrained food budgets in a Scandinavian welfare state context, *Social Policy and Society*, 14, 3, 429–42.

Nnakwe, N.E., 2008, Dietary patterns and prevalence of food insecurity among low-income families participating in community food assistance programs in a Midwest town, *Family and Consumer Sciences Research Journal*, 36, 3, 229–42.

OHCHR, 2014, *Ratification of 18 international human rights treaties*, http://indicators.ohchr.org/.

OHCHR, n.d., *Special Rapporteur on the Right to Food*, www.ohchr.org/EN/Issues/Food/Pages/FoodIndex.aspx.

Ollerenshaw, E., 2016, Three Years On: An Independent Review of Local Council Tax Support Schemes, Department for Communities and Local Government, https://www.gov.uk/government/publications/local-council-tax-support-schemes-an-independent-review.

Oxfam, 2013, *Food poverty in the UK*, http://policy-practice.oxfam.org.uk/our-work/inequality/food-poverty.

Padley, M. and Hirsch, D., 2014, *Households below a minimum income standard: 2008/9 to 2011/12*, Summary, York: Joseph Rowntree Foundation, www.jrf.org.uk/report/households-below-minimum-income-standard-20089-201112.

Pantazis, C., Gordon, D. and Levitas, R., 2006, *Poverty and social exclusion in Britain*, Bristol: Policy Press.

Pérez de Armiño, K., 2014, Erosion of rights, uncritical solidarity and food banks in Spain, in G. Riches and T. Silvasti (eds) *First World Hunger Revisited: Food charity or the right to food?* Basingstoke: Palgrave Macmillan, 131–45.

Perry, J., Sefton, T., Williams, M. and Haddad, M., 2014, *Emergency use only: Understanding and reducing the use of food banks in the UK*, Oxfam, http://policy-practice.oxfam.org.uk/publications/emergency-use-only-understanding-and-reducing-the-use-of-food-banks-in-the-uk-335731.

Pfeiffer, S., Ritter, T. and Hirseland, A., 2011, Hunger and nutritional poverty in Germany: quantitative and qualitative empirical insights, *Critical Public Health*, 21, 4, 417–28.

Pfeiffer, S., Ritter, T. and Oestreicher, E., 2015, Food insecurity in German households: qualitative and quantitative data on coping, poverty consumerism and alimentary participation, *Social Policy and Society*, 14, 3, 483–95.

Popke, J., 2006, Geography and ethics: everyday mediations through care and consumption, *Progress in Human Geography*, 30, 504–12.

Poppendieck, J., 1994, Dilemmas of emergency food: a guide for the perplexed, *Agriculture and Human Values*, Fall, 69–76.

Poppendieck, J., 1998, *Sweet charity? Emergency food and the end of entitlement*, New York: Penguin.

Poppendieck, J., 2014, Food assistance, hunger and the end of welfare in the USA, in G. Riches and T. Silvasti (eds) *First world hunger revisited: Food charity or the right to food?* Basingstoke: Palgrave Macmillan, 176–90.

PROOF (no date) Monitoring food insecurity in Canada, Fact sheet, http://proof.utoronto.ca/wp-content/uploads/2016/06/monitoring-factsheet.pdf.

PSE (Poverty and Social Exclusion), 2012, *Going backwards: 1983–2012*, www.poverty.ac.uk/pse-research/going-backwards-1983-2012.

Rambeloson, Z.J., Darmon, N. and Ferguson, E.L., 2007, Linear programming can help identify practical solutions to improve the nutritional quality of food aid, *Public Health Nutrition*, 11, 4, 395–404.

Register of All-Party Groups, 2014, Hunger and Food Poverty, 30 March, www.publications.parliament.uk/pa/cm/cmallparty/register/hunger-and-food-poverty.htm.

Richards, D. and Smith, M.J., 2002, *Governance and public policy in the UK*, Oxford: Oxford University Press.

Riches, G., 1997a, *First world hunger: Food security and welfare politics,* Basingstoke: Macmillan.

Riches, G., 1997b, Hunger, food security and welfare policies: issues and debates in first world societies, *Proceedings of the Nutrition Society*, 56, 63–74.

Riches, G., 1997c, Hunger, welfare and food security: emerging strategies, in G. Riches (ed.) *First world hunger: Food security and welfare politics*, Basingstoke: Macmillan, 165–78.

Riches, G., 1999, Advancing the human right to food in Canada: social policy and the politics of hunger, welfare, and food security, *Agriculture and Human Values*, 16, 203–11.

Riches, G., 2002, Food banks and food security: welfare reform, human rights and social policy: lessons from Canada?, *Social Policy & Administration*, 36, 6, 648–63.

Riches, G., 2011, Thinking and acting outside the charitable food box: hunger and the right to food in rich societies, *Development in Practice*, 21, 4–5, 768–75.

Riches, G. and Silvasti, T., 2014, *First world hunger revisited: Food charity or the right to food?* Basingstoke: Palgrave Macmillan.

Rocha, C., 2014, A right to food approach: public food banks in Brazil, in G. Riches and T. Silvasti (eds) *First world hunger revisited: Food charity or the right to food?*, Basingstoke: Palgrave Macmillan, 1–14.

Save the Children, 2012, *Child poverty in 2012: It shouldn't happen here*, Manchester: Save the Children, www.savethechildren.org.uk/sites/default/files/documents/child_poverty_2012.pdf.

Save the Children, 2013, *Enough food for everyone IF,* Manchester: Save the Children, www.savethechildren.org.uk/2013-01/enough-food-everyone-if.

Scott, J., 2001, *Power,* Cambridge: Polity.

Scottish Government, 2014, *Foodbank fund open for applications,* 2 June, http://news.gov.scot/news/foodbank-fund-open-for-applications.

Sen, A., 1983, Poor, relatively speaking, *Oxford Economic Papers,* 35, 153–69.

Sen, A., 1985, A sociological approach to the measurement of poverty: a reply to Professor Peter Townsend, *Oxford Economic Papers,* 37, 669–76.

Sen, A., 2004, Elements of a theory of human rights, *Philosophy and Public Affairs,* 32, 4, 317–56.

Sen, A., 2008, Why and how is health a human right? *The Lancet,* 372, 9655, 2010.

Sheffield City Council, n.d., *Council tax support,* www.sheffield.gov.uk/in-your-area/benefit/claimingbenefit/counciltaxsupport.html.

Shelter, 2013, *4 out of 10 families cut back on food to stay in their homes,* http://england.shelter.org.uk/news/march_2013/4_out_of_10_families_cut_back_on_food_to_stay_in_their_homes.

Silvasti, T. and Karjalainen, J., 2014, Hunger in a Nordic welfare state: Finland, in G. Riches and T. Silvasti (eds) *First World Hunger Revisited: Food charity or the right to food?* Basingstoke: Palgrave Macmillan, 72–86.

Silvasti, T. and Riches, G., 2014, Hunger and food charity in rich societies: what hope for the right to food?, in G. Riches and T. Silvasti (eds) *First world hunger revisited: Food charity or the right to food?* Hampshire: Palgrave Macmillan, 191–208.

Simmons, D., 2013, *What is replacing the social fund?* www.cpag.org.uk/content/what-replacing-social-fund.

Special Rapporteur on the Right to Food, n.d., *The human right to food,* www.ohchr.org/EN/Issues/Food/Pages/FoodIndex.aspx.

Sosenko, F., Livingstone, N. and Fitzpatrick, S., 2013, *Overview of food aid provision in Scotland,* Scottish Government, www.gov.scot/Resource/0044/00440458.pdf.

Tait, C., 2015, *Hungry for change: The final report of the Fabian Commission on Food and Poverty,* London: Fabian Society, http://foodandpoverty.org.uk/publication-hungry-for-change/

Tarasuk, V., 2001, A critical examination of community-based responses to household food insecurity in Canada, *Health Education & Behavior,* 28, 4, 487–99.

Tarasuk, V. and Eakin, J.M., 2003, Charitable food assistance as symbolic gesture: an ethnographic study of food banks in Ontario, *Social Science & Medicine*, 56, 1505–15.

Tarasuk, V. and Eakin, J.M., 2005, Food assistance through 'surplus' food: insights from an ethnographic study of food bank work, *Agriculture and Human Values*, 22, 177–86.

Taylor, A. and Loopstra, R., 2016, *Too poor to eat: Food insecurity in the UK*, Food Foundation, http://foodfoundation.org.uk/wp-content/uploads/2016/07/FoodInsecurityBriefing-May-2016-FINAL.pdf.

Taylor-Gooby, P. and Stoker, G., 2011, The Coalition programme: a new vision for Britain or politics as usual? *The Political Quarterly*, 82, 1, 4–15.

Townsend, P., 1979, *Poverty in the UK*, Middlesex: Pelican.

Townsend, P., 1985, A sociological approach to the measurement of poverty: a rejoiner to Professor Amartya Sen, *Oxford Economic Papers*, 37, 695–68.

Trussell Trust, 2010, *Jobcentres to give charity food vouchers to neediest clients*, press release, 20 December, www.trusselltrust.org/wp-content/uploads/sites/2/2015/06/PRESS-RELEASE-Jobcentre-to-give-out-food-vouchers.pdf.

Trussell Trust, 2011, *50% increase in UK people fed by charity foodbanks*, press release, 27 September, www.trusselltrust.org/wp-content/uploads/sites/2/2015/06/50percentIncreaseInNumbersFedbyFoodbanks.pdf.

Trussell Trust, 2013, *Increasing numbers turning to foodbanks since April welfare reforms*, press release, 11 July, www.trusselltrust.org/wp-content/uploads/sites/2/2015/06/Increasing-numbers-turning-to-foodbanks-since-Aprils-welfare-reforms-1.pdf.

Trussell Trust, 2016, *Foodbank use remains at a record high, as new data mapping tool gives fresh insights into UK hunger*, 15 April, www.trusselltrust.org/wp-content/uploads/sites/2/2015/06/Foodbank-use-remains-at-record-high.pdf.

Trussell Trust, n.d.a, *Trussell Trust foodbank stats*, www.trusselltrust.org/news-and-blog/latest-stats/.

Trussell Trust, n.d.b, *A response to inaccurate and misleading reports about The Trussell Trust*, www.trusselltrust.org/rumour-response.

Trussell Trust, n.d.c, *UK foodbanks*, www.trusselltrust.org/what-we-do/.

Turner, R. and Keen, R., 2015, 2016 Benefits Uprating, House of Common Library Briefing Paper, Number CBP 7410, 26 November, http://researchbriefings.parliament.uk/ResearchBriefing/Summary/CBP-7410#fullreport.

United Nations, 1966, *International Covenant on Economic, Social and Cultural Rights*, www.ohchr.org/EN/ProfessionalInterest/Pages/CESCR.aspx.

United Nations, n.d., *The Universal Declaration of Human Rights*, www.un.org/en/universal-declaration-human-rights/index.html.

Veit-Wilson, J., 2000, States of welfare: a conceptual challenge, *Social Policy and Administration*, 34, 1, 1–25.

Wallop, H., 2009, Thousands of people rely on food handouts as recession bites, *The Telegraph*, 26 May, www.telegraph.co.uk/finance/recession/5387484/Thousands-of-people-rely-on-food-handouts-as-recession-bites.html.

Watson, M. and Meah, A., 2013, Food, waste and safety: negotiating conflicting social anxieties into the practices of domestic provisioning, *The Sociological Review*, 60, S2, 102–20.

Webb, P., Coates, P., Frongillo, E.A., Lorge Rogers, B., Swindale, A. and Bilinsky, P., 2006, Measuring household food insecurity: why it's so important and yet so difficult to do, *The Journal of Nutrition*, 136, 5.

Williams, A. Cloke, P., May, J., and Goodwin, M., 2016, Contested space: the contradictory political dynamics of food banks in the UK, *Environment and Planning A*, doi: 10.1177/0308518X16658292.

Williams, F., 2001, In and beyond New Labour: towards a new political ethics of care, *Critical Social Policy*, 21, 467–93.

Williams, Z., 2013, Skivers v strivers: the argument that pollutes people's minds, *The Guardian*, 9 January, www.theguardian.com/politics/2013/jan/09/skivers-v-strivers-argument-pollutes.

Yu, M.L., Nebbitt, M. and Von, E., 2010, Food stamp program participation, informal supports, household food security and child food security: a comparison of African American and Caucasian households in poverty, *Children and Youth Services Review*, 32, 5, 767–73.

Ziegler, J., Golay, C., Mahon, C. and Way, S.A., 2011, *The fight for the right to food: Lessons learned*, Basingstoke: Palgrave Macmillan.

Index

References to figures are in *italics*